SHOP IMAGE GRAPHICS IN LONDON

ショップイメージ グラフィックス イン ロンドン

PIE
BOOKS

Shop Image Graphics in London

©2007 PIE BOOKS

PIE BOOKS
2-32-4 Minami-Otsuka, Toshima-ku, Tokyo
170-0005 Japan
Tel: +81-3-5395-4811 Fax: +81-3-5395-4812
http://www.piebooks.com
e-mail: editor@piebooks.com
        sales@piebooks.com

ISBN978-4-89444-583-3   Printed in Japan

FOREWORD

日本国内のショップアイデンティティを特集した『ショップ イメージグラフィックス』の初の海外編となる本書は、ロンド ンという一都市をまとめたことによって、都市の歴史がデザ インに深く関わり、デザインの傾向に影響を与えることがよ く現れている。

作品はジャンル別に紹介したが、デザインのテイストで分 けるならば、クラシック、モダン、そして異国文化のエスニック やオリエンタルという3つの特徴がみられる。

日本でいうと和風にあたるクラシックは、伝統的な装飾 文字や柄を使いながらも古くささを排し、洗練された色使 いや書体をアレンジすることによって、現代風によみがえら せている。Rococo Chocolates（p74）のパッケージは伝統 を重んじ、アンティークを愛する国ならではの美しさを感じ ることができる。

次に今や世界のモダンデザイン界をリードするテランス・ コンラン卿に始まるモダンデザインは、シンプルな書体や 色使いで、ホテルやレストラン、インテリアショップを都会的 なものにし、ロンドンをデザインの国と位置づけるのに重 要な役割をはたしている。

そして異国の文化が入ってくる機会が多かった歴史を 持つロンドンは、異国のものをロンドン風にアレンジして 見事に成功させている。すしバーのItsu（p92）は、外国人 からみた日本という国の色使いに、モダンなテイストをプ ラスさせることによって、新しいジャパニーズスタイルを 確立している。飲茶店のYauatcha（p76）やスパのCalmia （p178）もモダンなオリエンタルデザインが素晴らしい。

全てのショップがこのテイストとは言いきれないが、ロン ドンという都市の活気とデザイン性の高さはどのショップ からも感じ取ることができる。

最後になりましたが、本書制作にあたりご協力いただい たショップの方々、制作会社の方々にこの場を借りてお礼 申し上げます。

This volume, the first overseas edition of the Shop Image Graphics series that until now has showcased examples of Japanese shop identity, concentrates on a single city: London, and by doing so reveals the intimate connection between the city's history and the design on its streets, and how that history has influenced international design trends.

The examples here are presented by genre, however in terms of approach, are dominated by three broad design looks: classic, modern, and exotic, e.g. ethnic or Oriental. Classic, which in Japan corresponds to wafu or traditional Japanese style, employs traditional decorative text and patterns while simultaneously shedding any hint of old-fashioned and combining elegant colors and fonts to gain a new, modern lease of life. The packaging for Rococo Chocolates (p74) exudes the kind of beauty we've come to expect from a nation known for its respect for tradition and love of antiques.

Next, modern design, of which Britain's Sir Terence Conran is a leading international practitioner, uses simple fonts and color combinations to give hotels, restaurants and home furnishing stores an urban feel, and plays a vital part in London's reputation as a top design location.

In addition, as a city with a long history of absorbing and celebrating other cultures, the British capital succeeds in taking elements of those cultures and arranging them in uniquely London ways. The Itsu sushi bar (p92) for example combines colors that people in other countries associate with Japan with a modern look to create a totally new Japanese style, while the modern Oriental design of places like the Yauatcha dim sum restaurant (p76) and Calmia spa (p178) are also shining examples of modern Oriental design.

While not all London shops are fitted out in these styles, every shop in London does convey the vibrancy and sophisticated design values that characterize this great metropolis.

Finally, allow us to take this opportunity to thank the many people from the shops featured, and from the design and production companies involved, for their invaluable cooperation in the production of this book.

ピエ・ブックス編集部

The editors, PIE BOOKS

CONTENTS

LIVING

FOOD

FASHION

SERVICE

Editorial Notes

CREDIT FORMAT クレジットフォーマット

A.	ショップ名	Shop Name
B.	制作スタッフ・クレジット	Creative Stuff
C.	業種	Type of Business
D.	店舗所在地	Address
E.	ウェブサイト・アドレス	Web Site Address
F.	ショップ・コンセプト文	Shop Description

CREATIVE STUFF 制作スタッフクレジット

AF:	建築設計事務所	Architectual Firm
A:	ショップ設計者	Architect in Charge
CD:	クリエイティブ・ディレクター	Creative Director
AD:	アート・ディレクター	Art Director
D:	デザイナー	Designer
LD:	ロゴ・デザイナー	Logo Designer
P:	フォトグラファー	Photographer
I:	イラストレーター	Illustrator
CW:	コピーライター	Copywriter
DF:	グラフィック・デザイン事務所	Design Firm

＊上記以外の制作者呼称は省略せずに記載しております。
Full name of all others involved in the creation / production of the work.

＊本書に掲載されている店舗写真、販促ツール、商品、店名、住所などは、すべて2006年12月時点での情報になります。ご了承ください。
All in store-related information, including photography, promotional items, products, shop name, and address are accurate as of December 2006.

＊作品提供者の意向によりクレジット・データの一部を記載していないものがあります。
Please note that some credit data has been omitted at the request of the submittor.

LIVING

Designers Guild デザイナーズ・ギルド

CD:Tricia Guild   P:Kenichi Nakao

Furniture and Home Accessories
家具、ホームアクセサリー
▶ 267 Kings Road, London SW3 5EN
http://www.designersguild.com

Tester テスター

Envelope 封筒

Established in 1970 Designers Guild is a leading worldwide luxury home furnishing brand. Designers Guild designs and wholesales furnishing fabrics, wallcoverings, upholstery, bed and bath under the Designers Guild and other brands throughout Europe and worldwide. Our philosophy is to combine creativity and innovation with the highest levels of quality: quality of design, product, service and people.

1970年設立の世界的な大手メーカー。ファブリック、壁紙、室内装飾品、寝具、バス用品などを、デザイナーズギルド・ブランドをはじめ世界各国のブランドのもとでデザイン・販売しています。デザイン、製品、サービス、人……あらゆる面において、最高の質と創造性・革新性を融合することをブランド理念としています。

Pattern
The stunning new book
by Tricia Guild

Designers Guild

cushions

sarafan

sarafan turquoise

macinsky scarlet

montplaisir scarlet

montplaisir berry

montplaisir moss

montplaisir turquoise

montplaisir linen

montplaisir mandarin

valeriya moss

valeriya jade

valeriya fuchsia

khaskov scarlet

khaskov berry

khaskov moss

Catalog　カタログ

DESIGNERS GUILD paint

whitest

off white

frost

dove

cloud

lead

pebble

cypress

meadow

primrose

alchemilla

willow　NEW

fennel　NEW

moss　NEW

heather

lilac

porcelain

morning sky

speedwell

jodhpur

DESIGNERS GUILD paint

"I am absolutely delighted with this glorious new colour palette, which captures so perfectly the spirit of the Designers Guild philosophy."

Tricia Guild

chalk

DESIGNERS GUILD paint

Catalog　カタログ

DESIGNERS GUILD
autumn 2006 new collections

Catalog　カタログ

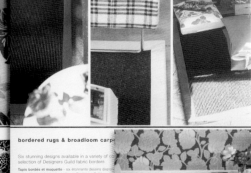

new zealand wool rugs

sarafan

DHR090/01
160cm x 260cm

bordered rugs & broadloom carpet

Six stunning designs available in a variety of colours, selection of Designers Guild fabric borders.

Tapis bordés et moquette - six étonnants dessins disponibles large selection de garnies en tissus Designers Guild.

Teppiche mit Bordüre & Auslegeware - sechs unterschiedliche Bordüre, sie haben eine Auswahl an verschiedenen Designers

Tappeti bordati & moquette - tappeti bordati e moquette

Alfombras con cenefa & moquetas - seis maravillosos

DESIGNERS GUILD
rugs & carpets autumn winter 2006

DESIGNERS GUILD bed & bath autumn winter 2006

Catalog　カタログ

Miller Harris ミラー・ハリス

A, AD, LD, Interior Design, Graphic Design:Ab Rogers Design　CD:Lyn Harris　P:Kenichi Nakao

Perfume
香水

▶ 21 Bruton Street, Mayfair, London W1J 6QD
http://www.millerharris.com

One of the overriding differences between Miller Harris and other fragrance houses is the luxurious style of both the products and the shops. One is inspired to use this company as a library of scent, there is not one fragrance that you will want to use exclusively. It is quite unusual to find a company that changes the way you feel about scent but Miller Harris does just that.

ミラーハリスの最大の特徴は、商品とショップの贅沢さです。香りの図書館として利用したくなるようなショップで、独り占めしたくなるフレグランスがいくつも見つかります。香りについての考え方を変えてしまうようなショップなどめったにありませんが、ミラーハリスこそ、まさにそんなショップです。

Tester テスター
Instruction 説明書

Post Card ポストカード

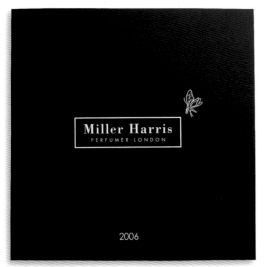

Catalog　カタログ

Philosophy

The foundation stone of the Miller Harris brand is precious ingredients. Lyn's unique style comes from her dedication to fragrance. She is unrepentant in her search for new materials, sourcing the best from around the world; iris from Florence, violet leaf from France, jasmin from Egypt, orange flower from Tunisia and sandalwood from the Pacific. All the fragrances used are the highest quality naturals available which give the soul and essence to all the Miller Harris scents. With these precious notes in her possession, her aim is always to preserve their delicacy so that they work in harmony creating works of art.

One of the overriding differences between Miller Harris and other fragrance houses is the luxurious style of both the products and the shops. One is inspired to use this company as a library of scent, there is not one fragrance that you will want to use exclusively, each one is representative of different moods, occasions, seasons and even times of the day. It is quite unusual to find a company that changes the way you feel about scent but Miller Harris does just that.

Fleur du Matin

100ml Eau de Parfum, 50ml Eau de Parfum, 200ml Shower Wash

Fleur du Matin is a clean, green, fresh and easy fragrance. This is ideal to travel with, when you arrive somewhere tired and need a spritz of something to revitalize. Inspired by the dew and floral/herbal scent of an early morning walk on the island of Porquerolles, it makes a fabulous scent for the spring and summer. It is a blend of the natural scents of the Provencal coast; pine, marjoram, honeysuckle and neroli with lemon and basil.

Noix de Tubéreuse

100ml Eau de Parfum, 50ml Eau de Parfum, 200ml Body Lotion, 125g Candle

Noix de Tubéreuse is a deep, sensuous and oriental take on this classic fragrance made from the endangered tuberose fields of Grasse. It is blended with mimosa, wild green clover and a little violet. What sets this tuberose apart from the others is its buttery note preventing it from becoming too heavy or cloying. It remains an intimidating, headstrong and powerful fragrance, a great signature scent for the modern, urban woman.

Penhaligon's ペンハリゴンズ

CD:Rosemary Rodriguez Packaging & Product Design:Ellen Knowles Interior Design:Nick Sheridan
A:CDL Retail Design & Project Management P:Kenichi Nakao, Akiko Watanabe

Perfume
香水
▶ 132 Kings Road, Chelsea, London SW3 4TR
http://www.penhaligons.co.uk/

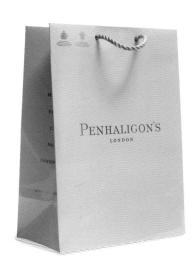

Instruction 説明書

Penhaligon's is the quintessential English house. It has always embodied essential English values that make it more than just a traditional house. Eccentricity, aristocracy, independence, wit and understated exuberance are the very core of Penhaligon's identity. The new concept behind the store goes back to the core values of English tradition and eccentric elegance, while giving it a modern interpretation.

典型的なイングリッシュ・ハウスでありながら、ただ伝統的というのではなく、英国の価値観の真髄を具現化したショップ。奇抜さ、上流階級、独立、ウィット、控えめな豊かさなどがペンハリゴンズの個性。ショップの新コンセプトは、英国の伝統とエキセントリックな気品を大切にしつつ、その価値観に新たな解釈を与えています。

Wrapping Paper
ラッピングペーパー

Korres Store コレス・ストア

Cosmetics
化粧品
▶ 124 King's Road, London
http://www.korres.com

A, Interior Design:Wells Mackereth Architects CD, LD, Graphic Design:Yiannis Kouroudis (K2 Design)
AD:Stavros Papayiannis (Staged Design) P:Kenichi Nakao

Package
パッケージ

Korres natural products is a Greek company with its roots in the oldest homeopathic pharmacy in Athens. Our King's Road store was the first stand-alone Korres boutique store. We have used custom made fixtures of clean white ceramic and solid timber, inspired by the product's fusion of nature with science.

コレス・ナチュラル・プロダクツは、ギリシャの企業で、アテネで最も歴史あるホメオパシー薬局に端を発しています。キングスロード店は、コレス初の路面店です。自然と科学の融合により生まれた商品をイメージし、清潔感のある白のセラミックと一枚板を用いて特別に製作した什器を使用しています。

Catalog カタログ

1 Cleansing
2 Hydration
   Perfection

Eyes and Lips

KORRES STOCKING FILLER

ATHENS

KORRES
NATURALPRODUCTS

LIMITED EDITION

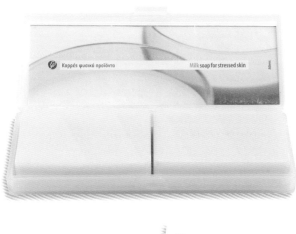

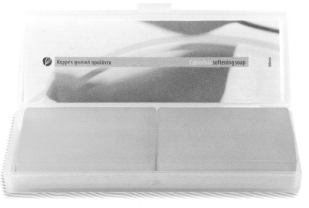

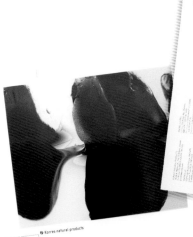

Catalog　カタログ

Korres natural products
www.korres.com

Athens

Athens

From Homeopathic remedies to natural products, Korres natural products is a Greek company with roots in the oldest Homeopathic Pharmacy of Athens. The first product of the Korres Pharmacy was a herbal throat pastille with honey and aniseed, a recipe inspired by "rakomelon", a warming spirit-with-honey concoction, which George Korres' grandfather used to favour in his hometown on the island of Naxos. The company offers today a complete skin, body and hair care range, sun care products and herbal preparations.

Korres Natural Products
20-26 K. Manou St. 116 33, Athens, Greece
+30 210 756 5800 F +30 210 756 2122 E info@korres.com
www.korres.com

KORRESNATURALPRODUCTS

ATHENS

KORRESNATURALPRODUCTS

On Wednesday **18th October** Korres Natural Products welcomes you to its flagship store:

Prepare for the party season with our **brand new instantly brightening & illuminating Wild Rose mask and brightening & line-smoothing Wild Rose face and eye serum**, both rich in radiance-boosting vitamin C to help fend off Winter blues and chase away tired-looking skin.

For all purchases of more than one Wild Rose brightening product receive a complimentary 5ml Wild Rose moisturizer (Our best-selling face care product and the first cosmetic preparation ever made by Korres Natural Products!)

Exclusive Christmas preview
Avoid last-minute Christmas shopping stress and allow us to provide: gift ideas and products suitable for the whole family gift-wrapping and mail-order / delivery services

Enjoy an exclusive discount up to 30% on selected best-selling sets!
We promise to keep your energy-levels up with nibbles and refreshments all the while!

DERMATOLOGICALLY TESTED
MINERAL OIL FREE
SILICONE FREE
PROPYLENE GLYCOL FREE
ETHANOLAMINE FREE

www.korres.com
Korres Natural Products
124 King's Road, Chelsea LONDON SW3 4TR
T 020 7581 6455 E info@korresstore.co.uk

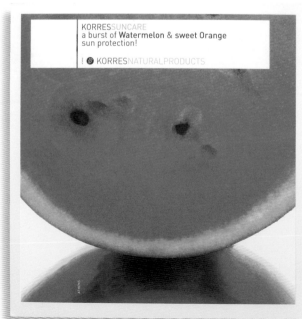

KORRESSUNCARE
a burst of **Watermelon** & sweet **Orange** sun protection!

KORRESNATURALPRODUCTS

ATHENS

KORRESSUNCARE

Come and experience a suncare range that will take you right back to your Summer Holidays in Greece! Mouth-watering sweet Orange and juicy Watermelon, make the range ripe with sun protective properties.

WATERMELON SUNSCREEN FACE CREAMS SPF 20 & SPF 30
SWEET ORANGE SUNSCREEN FACE & BODY MILK SPF 15 & SPF 20
YOGHURT COOLING GEL

Spring-Summer 2006

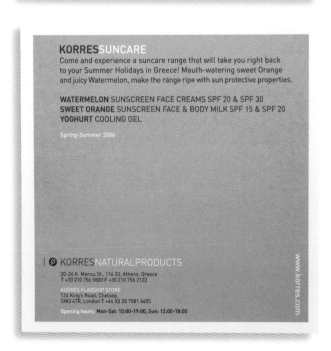

KORRESNATURALPRODUCTS
20-26 K. Manou St., 116 33, Athens, Greece
T +30 210 756 5800 F +30 210 756 2122

KORRES FLAGSHIP STORE
124 King's Road, Chelsea,
SW3 4TR, London T +44 (0) 20 7581 6455

Opening hours: Mon-Sat: 10:00-19:00, Sun: 12:00-18:00

www.korres.com

Catalog　カタログ

Catalog　カタログ

Catalog　カタログ

Stores

Product Range

Catalog　カタログ

Black Tulip

ブラックチューリップ

Florist and Design Boutique
花、雑貨

▶ 28 Exmouth Market Clerkenwell, London EC1R 4QE
http://www.theblacktulip.co.uk/

A, Interior Design:Paul Crofts   CD:Fiona Mackenzie-Jenkin   LD, Graphic Design:Micha Weidmann
P:Akiko Watanabe

1681
Carthusia
I Profumi di Capri

IO
"CAPRI"
EAU DE PARFUM

PRODOTTO NELL'ISOLA DI CAPRI

Gift Box
ギフトボックス

Clerkenwell
Telephone 020 7689 0068
Fax 020 7689 0204
enchant@theblacktulip.co.uk
www.theblacktulip.co.uk

28 Exmouth Market
Clerkenwell, London EC1R 4QE
Telephone 020 7689 0068
Fax 020 7689 0204
enchant@theblacktulip.co.uk
www.theblacktulip.co.uk

Letterhead　レターヘッド

'The tulip is supreme amongst flowers in the same way that humans are lords of the animals, diamonds eclipse all other precious stones, and the sun rules the stars.'
Charles de la Chesnee Monstereul

the black tulip

Flyer　フライヤー

the black tulip precipitating an aesthetic renaissance.

Speak with us on 020 7689 0068 write to enchant@theblacktulip.co.uk or visit at 28, Exmouth Market, Clerkenwell, London EC1R 4QE where we shall be delighted to assist you further.

Engage at www.theblacktulip.co.uk and join our diary service

...t in the heart of Clerkenwell's ...th Market The Black Tulip ...s offering a sensory sensation ...our, scent and form.

...tyle sumptuous floral displays ...ll occasions, uniting this service ...a miscellany of hothouse plants, ...gside complementary gifts of ...usive perfume for the body and ...ne, beautiful ceramics and glass-...re. Come start your affair...

Leaflet　リーフレット

28 Exmouth Market
Clerkenwell, London EC1R 4QE
Telephone 020 7689 0068
Fax 020 7689 0204
enchant@theblacktulip.co.uk
www.theblacktulip.co.uk

Shop Card　ショップカード

The Black Tulip, whose title was inspired by the Alexandre Dumas novel of C17th tulip bulb trading, specialises in the supply of high quality, unusual fashion focused flowers sold alongside complementary products spanning perfume, glassware, ceramics, antiques and on-off design items all based around a floral theme.

17世紀のチューリップの球根取引をテーマにしたアレクサンドル・デュマの小説『ブラック・チューリップ』が名前の由来。花をモチーフにした、高品質で個性的な服飾品をはじめ、香水、ガラス製品、陶磁器から、アンティーク品、1点もののデザインアイテムなど、花にまつわる商品ばかりを集めた専門店です。

Farrow & Ball ファロウ&ボール

Paint and Wallpaper
ペンキ、壁紙
▶ 38 Cross Street, Islington, London N1 2BG
http://www.farrow-ball.com

A, CD, AD, LD, Sales & Marketing Director, Interior Design, Graphic Design:Sarah Cole   P:Akiko Watanabe

Application　申し込み用紙

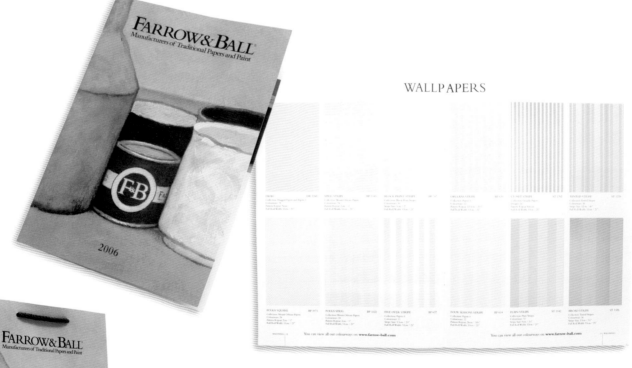

Farrow & Ball manufacture 100% of the paint and wallpaper they sell. Producing unrivalled colours, using only the finest ingredients, Farrow & Ball still make paint and wallpaper by traditional methods to original formulations. With over 130 paint colours available in 13 finishes, and over 700 wallpaper colourways in stris, stripes and patterned papers, the choice is virtually unlimited.

ファロー＆ボールが扱う塗料や壁紙はすべて自社製品。最高の原料のみを使用し、他にはない色合いを生みだしているこの店では、伝統的な方法により、オリジナル塗料を製造。塗料は13種類130色以上、壁紙は各種ストライプや柄物などがあり、カラーバリエーションは700以上という、まさに無限ともいえる品揃えです。

Bliss ブリス

CD, AD, D, I:In House   P:Akiko Watanabe

Spa and Beauty Products
スパ、ビューティー用品
▶ 60 Sloane Avenue, Chelsea, London SW3 3DD
www.blisslondon.co.uk

Beauty matters, absolutely - but doesn't absolutely matter. Bliss provides a comprehensive and results focused menu of services for women who need effective treatments in a fun, calm and friendly atmosphere.

もちろん美しさはとても重要な要素です。とはいえ、それがすべてではありません。ブリスは、楽しく静かでフレンドリーな雰囲気の中、効果的なトリートメントを受けたいという女性向けに、結果に焦点を当てた各種メニューを取り揃え、包括的なサービスを提供しています。

Wrapping Paper
ラッピングペーパー

bliss™

ow
stella
got her
mooth
back

lucing **steep clean**
eating body polish

bliss

triple oxygen™
instant energizing
mask

with vitamin C, fluidO₂™, NaPCA, and
EUK-134™ free-radical resisters

• engineered as a stand-in for our
  best world famous triple oxygen
  facial treatment
• renews oxygen molecules
  and detoxifiers
• a super-quick fix for dull, tired,
  celtic skin

super-strength skincare from
bliss, new york's hottest spa

e:100 mL/3.4 fl oz

bliss

clog-dissolving
cleansing milk™

fabulous milky wash
for all skin types

• exfoliating enzymes prevent
  blackhead buildup
• skin brightening bioflavonoids
  and grapeseed extract
• dual function face wash
  and 5-minute mask

super-strength skincare from
bliss, new york's hottest spa

8.28 fl oz/245 ml

bliss

super-eucalyptus
smoother

pre-shower body
softening mask

Catalog
カタログ

Diptyque ディプティーク

Candles and Perfume キャンドル、香水

▶ 195 Westbourne Grove, Notting Hill,
London W11 2SB
http://www.diptyqueparis.com

A, Interior Design:Blue Shy Hospitality   CD, AD, Graphic Design:Yves Coueslant   LD:Desmond Knox-Leet   P:Kenichi Nakao

Shop Card
ショップカード

Sticker
ステッカー

Press Release　プレスリリース
Letterhead　レターヘッド

Diptyque is a French parfumeur, originally based in Paris. We create simple and beautiful perfumes and scented candles, using natural essences and oils in very high concentrations. Our creations are as close to Nature as possible.

パリで創業したフランスのパフュームブランド、ディプティーク。たいへん純度の高いナチュラル・エッセンスやアロマオイルを使用した、シンプルで美しい香水やアロマキャンドルを作っています。ディプティークは、できるだけ自然に近い形でのものづくりにこだわったブランドです。

Catalog カタログ

EAU DE LIERRE
Anno 2006

Tuberose, Turkish rose, orange blossom leaf, rose berries, white musk, iris
Do son, a small town by the seaside in the Tonkin region, North of Indochina. The evening breeze carries, along with the seaside exhalation, the scent of flowers and tuberose.

Feuilles de lierre, cyclamen, géranium, poivre vert, ambre gris, palissandre, muscs
Le lierre, en Egypte, symbolisait la vie éternelle, chez les Grecs la joie et la vitalité; les Romains l'ont dédié à Bacchus et à la gloire des poètes; au Moyen-Age il signifiait la fidélité et l'amitié chevaleresque.

Ivy leaves, cyclamen, geranium, green pepper, ambergris, palissander wood, musks
In Egypt, ivy symbolized eternal life, in Greece joy and vitality; Romans used it to worship Bacchus and in honour of poets; in the Middle Ages it meant loyalty and chivalrous friendship.

DIPTYQUE

Eau de toilette
50 ml - 100 ml - 200 ml   80°   *1.7 fl.oz - 3.4 fl.oz - 6.8 fl.oz*

L'EAU
Anno 1968

Cannelle, rose, clou de girofle, géranium, santal
Basée sur une recette de pot pourri du 16ᵉ siècle et sur le parfum d'un pomander aux clous de girofle.

Cinnamon, rose, clove, geranium, sandalwood
Based on a 16th century pot pourri and a clove pomander.

L'AUTRE
Anno 1973

Coriandre, cardamome, patchouli, carvi, poivre, cumin, noix muscade

Un mélange sec et sensuel d'épices du Proche-Orient.

Coriander, cardamom, patchouli, carvi, pepper, cumin, nutmeg

A very dry and sensual blend of Near Eastern spices.

L'EAU TROIS
Anno 1975

Myrrhe, myrte, encens, ciste, pin, laurier, thym, romarin, origan
Le parfum des buissons résineux au long des côtes montagneuses du nord de la Grèce.

Myrrh, myrtle, incense, cistus, pine, laurel, thyme, rosemary, oregano
The resinous scent of aromatic shrubs from the mountainous coastline of northern Greece.

L'OMBRE DANS L'EAU
Anno 1983

Sève de feuille de cassis et rose de Bulgarie

Le parfum d'un jardin vert au bord de l'eau.

Blackcurrant leaf and Bulgarian rose

The scent of a green riverside garden.

EAU LENTE
Anno 1986

Opopanax, cannelle, épices indiennes

Basée sur l'évocation de parfum en usage à l'époque d'Alexandre le Grand.

Opopanax, Indian spices, cinnamon

Based on a description of scents used at the time of Alexander the Great.

Vinaigre de toilette
100 ml - 200 ml   80°   *3.4 fl.oz - 6.8 fl.oz*

Notre vinaigre de toilette, basé sur une recette du 19ᵉ siècle, contient une infusion de plantes, de bois et d'épices. Il peut être utilisé de plusieurs façons:
dans le bain il repose et rafraîchit le corps, adoucit la peau et la laisse discrètement parfumée. (Doser selon la quantité d'eau, le contenu d'un bouchon, ou plus).
Après un shampooing quelques gouttes dans l'eau de rinçage laissent les cheveux doux, brillants et légèrement parfumés.
Quelques gouttes sur le visage humide après rasage, ou sur le corps après la douche, rafraîchissent et tonifient la peau.
Pour rafraîchir et assainir l'air d'une pièce, mettre une cuillerée de vinaigre de toilette dans un bol et verser un peu d'eau bouillante.

Our toilet vina... a 19th centu... steeped in ex... plants, woods... It can be used... in the bath... refreshes the b... the skin & lea... scented. (One... more, accordin... and quantity... hair rinse after... drops in the... will soften, bri... scent the hair... As an after... drops in the ri... body friction... a face cloth o... will tonify & t... A spoonful o... in a bowl scal... water will fre... remove smell... tobacco.

Heal's ヒールズ

P:Yuki Sugiura

Furniture and Interior　家具、インテリア

▶ The Heal's Building 196 Tottenham Court Road, London W1T 7LQ
http://www.heals.co.uk

HEAL'S WEDDING & GIFT LIST

Create and manage your list in store on line or by phone.

Our gift to you...5% of your list back in gift vouchers*

Free delivery of your gifts*

Unrivalled range of furniture and homewares

Easy for family and friends to choose from your list

www.heals.co.uk/giftlist

*Conditions apply

HEAL'S HOUSE

INTRODUCING HEAL'S HOUSE, A COLLECTION DESIGNED WITH HOME ESSENTIALS IN MIND

THIS AFFORDABLE RANGE OFFERS CONTEMPORARY STYLE WITHOUT COMPROMISING ON QUALITY OR DESIGN.

THE HEAL'S HOUSE COLLECTION WILL NEVER BE DISCOUNTED, ENSURING OUTSTANDING QUALITY AND STYLE FOR LESS 100% OF THE TIME.

Heal's has been at the forefront of stylish, contemporary design ever since it opened its first store nearly 200 years ago. Heal's stocks only the very best in modern furniture and home accessories. Most items are exclusive to Heal's, all share the high quality workmanship and attention to detail for which our name is so well known.

1号店がオープンしてから約200年の間、スタイリッシュで現代的なデザインの最先端を走ってきたヒールズ。最高のモダン家具とホームアクセサリーのみを扱っています。ここでしか買えないものも多く、どの商品にも最高の職人技と細部への配慮が見られます。ヒールズは、そうした質の高さで知られるショップです。

Terre d'Oc テールドック

CD:Valerie Roubaud, Patrick Lions   P:Kenichi Nakao

Home Fragrance
アロマ用品
▶ 26 Marylebone High Street, London SW1 4PJ
http://www.terredoccreations.com

Terre d'oc was founded in 1995 with the aim of joining the perfumes of Grasse with exotic incenses from the Orient to create a unique collection of home perfumes whose fragrances are rooted in our deepest memories. Our range includes incense sticks, cones, room sprays, candles, perfume extracts and cappilla.

フランス、グラース地方の香水と東洋のエキゾチックなお香を組み合わせ、記憶の奥深くに刻まれたなつかしい香りを放つユニークなホームフレグランスを提供することを目指して1995年に創業。インセンススティックやコーン、ルームスプレー、キャンドル、フレグランスオイル、カッピーラなどを取り揃えています。

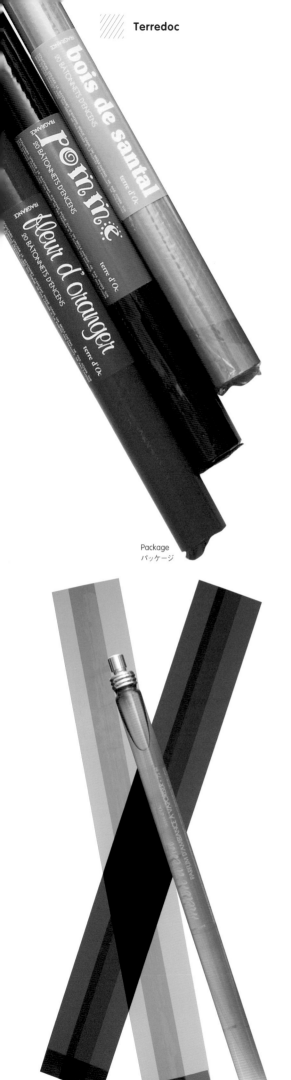

Package
パッケージ

Wild at Heart

ワイルド・アット・ハート

CD:Nikki Tibbles P:Akiko Watanabe

Florist and Homeware
花、生活雑貨
▶ 49a Ledbury Road, London W11 2AA
http://www.wildatheart.com

Match　マッチ

Card　カード

Live Wild at Heart opened in November 2005 and is an interiors and lifestyle boutique stocking fabulous designer pieces as well as vintage pieces. Furniture and paintings sit alongside Jonathan Adler, Cece Lepage, Sonia Rykiel and Karen Nicol as well as Live Wild at Heart scented candles.

2005年11月にオープンしたインテリア＆ライフスタイル・ブティック。優れたデザイナーアイテムをはじめ、ビンテージ商品も取り揃えています。家具や絵画の隣にはジョナサン・アドラー、チェチェ・ルパージュ、ソニア・リキエル、カレン・ニコルがデザインした商品やオリジナルのアロマキャンドルが並んでいます。

Fresh Line フレッシュ・ライン

Fresh Homemade Cosmetic
ハンドメイド化粧品

▶ 55 Kings Road, Chelsea, London SW3 4ND
http://www.freshline.gr

CD:Mayra Vagionis D, LD:In-House

Fresh Line

Fresh Homemade Cosmetics

Fresh Line

Catalog　カタログ

Breakfast

Body Breakfast:
A luscious breakfast for your body

A sumptuous breakfast with no calories!
As breakfast is the most basic meal of the day,
the products you use in your morning shower
are equally important and they often determine
your mood for the whole day!

On Fresh Line's breakfast buffet, you will find dishes made out of pure ingredients, crafted with imagination and love. Ask to see our great variety of marmalade, butter, whipped cream, sorbets, and mousse, to turn your morning routine into a feast of the senses... Everything is sold by weight and you may buy as much as you wish.

BODY CLEANSING
Strawberry Marmalade Bath Yummy...sweet drop on your loofah will offer you a dreamy morning shower or a fresh fragrant bath. It contains fresh strawberry juice!
Lemon and Ginger Marmalade Bath Lemon for extra cleansing and ginger essential oil for energy! The most revitalizing morning shower!
Vanilla Bath Wash with the comforting and fragrant vanilla bath and get in a romantic mood. This fragrance is perfect for romantic individuals.

Poseidon

The emerald blue of the Aegean sea, the salted sea air awakening your senses, and you sailing away... in your bathtub!
A fantastic line of unisex fragrance with rejuvenating and deodorant essential oils. Bergamot, fennel, cedarwood, iris, japanese sandalwood, lavender, sea salt, and palmarosa.
The line includes:
● Mega fizzy ball
● Soap by weight
● Sea world energizing shower gel (with thin jojoba grains for exfoliation).
● Sea world body milk
● Sea world body mist
● Aromatic wax tablet
● Air freshener

SANDALWOOD
Its chemical structure makes it a perfect skin remedy. It soothes, heals lesions, and relieves itchiness and allergies; moisturizes dry and dehydrated skin which makes wrinkles less visible. It is not only a strong anti-bacterial and deodorant but also acts as an after shave balm. If you apply a few drops on a lesion, it will heal soon. Generally, it is ideal for mature and problem skin. At the same time, it relaxes, unwinds, and puts you in a great mood. It helps an introvert person open up. It facilitates mutual understanding and alleviates possible insecurities. It stimulates the senses and the spirit. At Fresh Line, we use sandalwood in the Olympian Zeus, Poseidon, and Hera lines. Sandalwood is also a component of other aromatic formulas. It is available in pure essential oil form of 10 ml.

Fresh Line: A new Era

1994-2004
We have completed a decade of business and creative effort.
We introduced revolutionary ideas to the existing conservative cosmetics market.
We established a new lifestyle through the usage of our products.
We have gained a lot of fans and loyal friends.
We have the envy of our competitors.
We were recognized, nevertheless, as successful pioneers and innovators.
Experience and knowledge marks the first cycle, the first era, of Fresh Line.

2005
The new Fresh Line era has started with a new message:
Renewal, renaissance, renovation, growth.
Renewal of all our products: We have expanded our product range sixfold.
The renaissance of our recipes: They are more specialized, more therapeutic, and totally bioresearched.
Renewal of shapes, colours and forms: They are completely different, more artistic, more imaginative, more impressive, and much more dramatic.
Renovation of the setting: We have changed our decor and transformed our space into self service beauty bars.
Growth: We have crossed the borders, opened Fresh Line stores abroad, and earned international recognition.

We are celebrating our 10th birthday...
...and, as we move on, we promise:
We will continue to work tirelessly aiming for the highest quality.
We will continue and continue to be leaders, leaving others behind.
We will fulfill our wildest imagination.
We will renew ourselves and transform meeting the comfort of routine.
We will continue to be imitated, but we won't mind, because this proves we are the best.
We will continue to make logos in the international market and promote our Greek origin proudly. Greek writing and history will travel throughout the world in our stores.

Founded by Mayra Vagionis, Fresh Line now has stores in 6 different countries including the UK and its home base, Greece. We believe in making our own fresh products by hand, designing and printing our own labels and producing our own unique and delicate fragrances, not strong smells. We believe in romantic candlelit baths, sensual massage and filling every house with an appealing and relaxing aroma.

マイラ・ヴァジオニスが創業したフレッシュラインは、ギリシア本店のほか、英国など各国に6店舗を展開。手作りの商品、オリジナルのラベル、繊細で優しい独自の香り、がブランドの信条です。ろうそくを灯したロマンティックなバス、官能的なマッサージ、リラックスできる魅力的な香りで家を満たすことにこだわっています。

Penelope

Body Milk

esh Homemade Cosmetics

Fresh
Line

Poseidon

Sea World
Aromatherapy Body Milk

Fresh Homemade Cosmetics

Fresh
Line

Persephone

Ylang-Ylang and Jasmine
Aromatherapy Body Milk

Fresh Homemade Cosmetics

Fresh
Line

Orpheus
&
Eurydice

Vanilla and Mask
Relaxing Body Milk

Fresh Homemade Cosmetics

Fresh
Line

Skin
Regenarating
Oil mix

ΑΘΗΝΑ

Fresh
Line

Olive Oil Night Cream

Fresh Homemade Cosmetics

ΑΜΦΙΤΡΙΤΗ

Fresh
Line

Lemon and Seaweeds
Face Cream

Fresh Homemade Cosmetics

ΟΛΥΜΠΙΟΣ

Fresh
Line

Eye and face

Fresh Homemade

HERA

Fresh
Line

Eye cream with vitamin
Fresh Homemade Cosmetics

Cowshed カウシェッド

Cosmetic, Spa and Cafe 化粧品、スパ、カフェ

119 Portland Road, Clarendon Cross,
▶ London W11 4LN
http://www.cowshedclarendoncross.com

Interior Design:Ilse Crawford A:Michaelis Boyd Graphic Design:Sarah Pidgeon CD:Shaun Bowen, Karen Welman
LD:Pearlfisher I:Nina Chakrabarti

Created to enhance the ambience of personal pampering and social grooming, top quality treatments whilst enjoying a friendly homely feel of a warm kitchen that also provides home cooked foods and drinks. The Cowshed range is a collection of 100% vegetarian products, designed by Pearlfisher based on the concept of wallpapers adorning Babington House made using hand picked herbs from the walled garden there in Somerset, England.

自分だけの贅沢な時間や交流の場を素敵に演出するための場所。最高のトリートメントはもちろん、家庭的な温かいレストランで手作りの食事も楽しめます。商品はサマセットの庭園で手摘みされたハーブを用いた100%植物性。パッケージはバビントン・ハウスを彩る壁紙をモチーフにパールフィッシャーがデザインしています。

Brissi ブリッシイ

Lifestyle
生活雑貨
▶ 352 King's Road, Chelsea, London SW3 5UU
http://www.brissi.co.uk

CD, AD, Interior Design:Arianna Brissi & Siobhan Mckeating   LD:Brissi   P:Kenichi Nakao

Described by some as 'a blend of Parisian elegance and homely New England styling', Brissi is like a walk through your home as you travel through our living room, kitchen, bedroom and bathroom. With its light and airy interior, Brissi has exquisite finds for every aspect of home life, all displayed in a unique inspirational setting.

パリの気品とニューイングランドの家庭的なスタイルの融合、と評されたブリッシイ。我が家を歩いているような感覚でリビング、キッチン、ベッドルーム、バスルームを見て回ることができます。明るく開放的な店内には、暮らしのあらゆる場面に合わせた素敵な商品がユニークにディスプレイされ、多くのヒントを与えてくれます。

Pout パウト

Cosmetic
化粧品

▶ 32 Shelton Street, London WC2H 9JE
http://www.pout.co.uk

A, Interior Design:Angus Pond Associates and Chantal Laren
CD, AD, LD, Graphic Design:Chantal Laren (One of the founders of Pout) P:Kenichi Nakao

Shop Card　ショップカード

Post Card　ポストカード

Pout - the fabulously feminine, celebrity adored make-up brand from London was created by three spirited and ambitious women, Emily, Anna and Chantal. Pout offers sophistication and feminity to make women feel inspired and indulged, combining product formulations that delight & deliver with deliciously frivolous detail.

セレブにもファンの多いパウトは、元気いっぱいの意欲的な3人の女性、エミリー、アンナ、シャンタルが立ち上げた、とてもフェミニンなロンドン発のコスメ・ブランド。使い心地が良く効果の高い化粧品を、キュートなパッケージで提供しています。女心をくすぐり、満足させる、セクシーで洗練されたブランドです。

Catalog　カタログ

VV Rouleaux ヴィ・ヴィ・ルーロー

Ribbons, Trimmings and Braids
リボン、装飾品、ブレード
▶ 6 Marylebone High Street, London W10 4NJ
http://www.vvrouleaux.com

D, LD, CW, Interior Design:Annabel Lewis   AD:Rachel Washington   P:Kenichi Nakao

In 1990 Annabel Lewis closed her flower shop in Parsons Green and opened a specialist ribbon shop - V V Rouleaux. In 15 years, it has grown from a niche shop in Parsons Green to the most creative ribbons and trimmings company in Europe with its own retail shops, Trade Vaults, and design offices.

1990年、アナベル・ルイスはパーソンズ・グリーンにあった花屋を閉店し、リボン専門店ヴィ・ヴィ・ルーローをオープン。地元の小さなショップであったのが、15年の間にクリエイティブなリボンと装飾品を扱う企業トレード・ヴォールツにまで成長し、今ではヨーロッパに複数の支店とデザインオフィスをもっています。

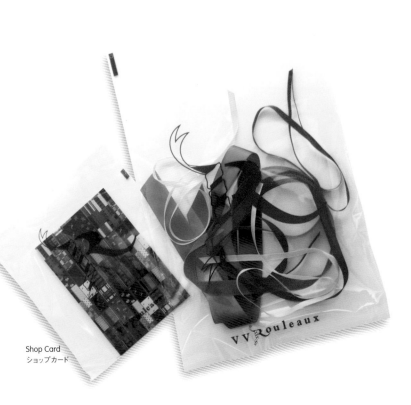

Shop Card
ショップカード

Shopping Bag
ショッピングバッグ

Santa Maria Novella

サンタ・マリア・ノヴェッラ

Perfumery and Pharmacy
香水、調剤薬局

▶ 117 Walton Street, London SW3 2HP
http://www.smnovella.it

A, Interior Design:Alessandro Manfredini   LD:Mediceo Family   P:Akiko Watanabe

Santa Maria Novella is an oasis rich in history and tradition where high standards are kept through limited, controlled production, using top quality natural raw materials and following manual procedures which have non changed since the Middle Ages.

サンタ・マリア・ノヴェッラは豊かな歴史と伝統をもつ安らぎの空間。最高品質の自然な原料を使用し、中世から変わらず守り通されている手作業での製造工程により、管理の下、限定数しか作られないため、高い品質が保たれています。

Tester　テスター

Farmacia Santa Maria Novella

117 Walton Street - London SW3 2HP   Tel: 020 7460 6600 Fax: 020 7460 6601

Mungo & Maud マンゴ&モード

A:Seth Stein CD, D:Nicola Sacher P:Akiko Watanabe

Dog and Cat Outfitters
犬、猫用品
▶ 79 Elizabeth street, London SW1W 9PJ
http://www.mungoandmaud.com

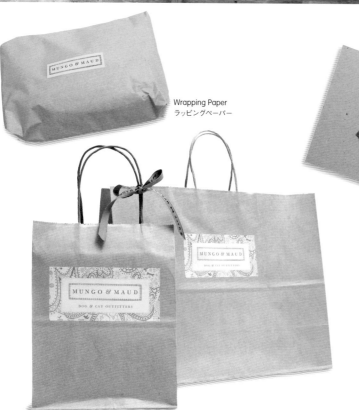

Wrapping Paper
ラッピングペーパー

Shop Card
ショップカード

Mungo & Maud was founded with the aim of creating stylish accessories for dogs, cats and their owners. The design approach is minimalist yet tactile, with a strong use of natural materials such as cotton, wool, leather and linen. Products range from hand-stitched leather collars and leads to hand-thrown feeding bowls, canvas beds and organic treats made to Mungo & Maud's own recipe.

犬や猫、そして飼い主のためのお洒落なアクセサリーを作る店として創業したマンゴ＆モード。デザインはミニマルで心地よく、綿、ウール、レザー、リンネルなど自然素材にこだわっています。手縫いのレザー製首輪やリード、キャンバス地のベッド、手製のボウル、特製レシピによるオーガニックフードなど品揃え豊富です。

Family Tree ファミリーツリー

Homeware, Clothing and Accessories
生活雑貨、洋服、アクセサリー
▶ 53 Exmouth Market, London EC1R 4QL
http://www.familytreeshop.co.uk

Interior Design:Matt & Takako Copeland LD, Graphic Design:Takako Copeland P:Brent Darby

Thank you for choosing "Washi Lamp"
"Washi Lamp" releases an elegant light
using the pattern of the print.
Washi is a traditional Japanese rice paper.
We have selected hand printed washi with
stencil method from a small artisan in Kyoto.
Print patterns are taken from kimono fabrics
of the late 19th century.
Washi is known for its strength; even sliding
doors and umbrellas are made out of washi
paper traditionally. The design of our products
are very simple in order to merge these striking
prints with modern living spaces.

＊Please use right wattage bulb for your
lamps/shades. They can be fitted with low
energy bulbs.

www.familytreeshop.co.uk

Leaflet　リーフレット

We wanted to create a cozy space where people gather.
As if inviting customers into our home. All the interior
work and graphics are "home made". Some shelving is
made from recycled floor boards. We stamp our logo- a
Victorian initial F, to shopping bags to create a bespoke
feel to complement our products.

我が家にお客様を招待するように、人が集まる温かい空
間をつくりたいとの思いで店づくりに取り組みました。
内装とグラフィックはすべて手作り。棚のいくつかは古
い床板をリサイクルしたものです。ビクトリア時代の書
体Fがモチーフのロゴをスタンプしたショッピングバッ
グが、商品の魅力をよりいっそう引き立たせます。

Cath Kidston キャス・キッドソン

Homeware, Clothing and Accessories
生活雑貨、洋服、アクセサリー
▶ 28 – 32 Shelton Street, London WC2H
http://www.cathkidston.co.uk

A, Interior Design, Graphic Design:In House   CD:Cath Kidston   AD:Andy Luckett   P:Kenichi Nakao

One of Britain's leading and most loved designers, Cath Kidston is best known for her vintage inspired prints for the home. It is one of the few truly original companies to come out of the home market in the last ten years, kick-starting the current trend for vintage chic.

英国を代表する人気デザイナーのひとりキャス・キッドソン。ビンテージ生地に着想を得たインテリア・ファブリックが最も有名です。過去10年間、イギリス国内の市場を勝ち抜いてきた数少ない個性的なオリジナルブランドのひとつで、今流行っているビンテージ・シックの火付け役となったブランドです。

Cath Kidston®

Autumn 2006

0870 850 1084
www.cathkidston.co.uk

Catalog　カタログ

www.cathkidston.co.uk

WASHED TOTES £25
Enzyme washed cotton tote bags,
fully lined with dual internal pockets.
Size 39 x 41cm. From left:
antique rose putty (81-52-4-2)
gypsy red (81-9-4-1)
posy cream (81-16-4-1)
summer blossom stone (81-14-4-1)
£25 each.

18

BAGS

WEEKEND BAG
Our classic oilcloth weekend bag in a generous shape and size, ideal for escaping for a weekend away or great as a sports bag. Size 49 x 33 x 14cm.

star red
(81-153-3-4) £60

star blue
(81-153-3-4) £60

gypsy red
(81-9-3-2) £60

mini cowboy
(81-152-3-5) £60

19

tel: 0870 850 1084

CHINTZ
Our much loved Chintz china. Practical
earthenware ideal for everyday.

Available as a 30 piece boxed set (6 dinner
plates, 6 side plates, 6 cups & saucers &
6 rimmed bowls) (20-108-68-7) £130
breakfast cup (20-108-68-3) £4
saucer (20-108-68-4) £2.50
dinner plate 27cm (20-108-68-1) £6
rimmed soup bowl 22cm (20-108-68-2) £6
side plate 21cm (20-108-68-5) £5
dipper bowl 12cm (20-108-68-6) £3.50

MUGS
Fine china mugs to mix an
1) boat classic mug (20-1

Twentytwentyone

トゥウェンティ・トゥウェンティ・ワン ▶

Interior
インテリア

274 Upper St, London N1
http://www.twentytwentyone.com/

A, Interior Design:Barber Osgerby Associates - Universal Directors:Tony Cunningham & Simon Alderson P:Akiko Watanabe

Robin Day

Tricorne tray
designed by Robin Day

Lucien Day

Pure linen teatowel
designed by Lucienne Day

Shop Card　ショップカード

Formed in 1993 by Simon Alderson and Tony Cunningham, to source and sell original modern furniture, lighting and industrial design. The mission was and still is to make people aware of good design and to select timeless high quality products that remain aesthetically pleasing and functional for years to come.

1993年にサイモン・オルダーソンとトニー・カニンガムが設立したショップで、オリジナルのモダン家具、照明、インダストリアル・デザインを扱っています。優れたデザインを人々に紹介し、時代に流されない機能性と美しさを兼ね備えた上質な製品をセレクトするという役割は、設立当初から今も変わっていません。

Bath Store バス・ストア

A,Interior Design:Adam Richards Architects   P:Akiko Watanabe

Bath Store バス用品

▶ Bathstore Islington, 33 Essex Road,
Islington, London N1 2SA
http://www.bathstore.com

The concept provides customers with a new and stimulating environment in a sector that has traditionally relied on fully-tiled 'room sets'. The design avoids these subjective distractions placing customers in an abstract bubble of colour to allow total focus on the products, all the while presenting tantalizing glimpses of new spaces, rooms and products.

コンセプトは、これまで総タイル張りの「ルームセット」に頼っていたバスルーム業界において、斬新で刺激的な空間を提供すること。既成概念にとらわれないデザインとし、カラフルで自由なディスプレイが商品を引き立たせます。お客様の興味をかき立てるような方法で、新しいスペース、バスルーム、製品を提案しています。

Delivery Pamphlet
配達パンフレット

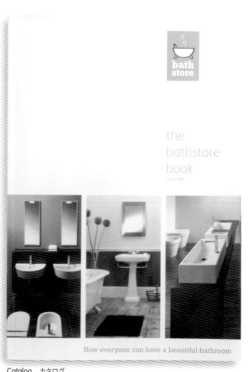

Catalog　カタログ

Cass Art

キャス・アート

A,Interior Architecture:William Russel (Pentagram)　CD:Mark Cass　P:Akiko Watanabe

Arts and Crafts Materials

アート、工芸用品

▶ 66-67 Colebrooke Row, London N1 8AB
http://www.cass-arts.co.uk

Shop Card
ショップカード

Discount Coupon
割引券

The largest art materials emporium in London, Cass Art is dedicated to finding customers the best range of quality fine art materials at very affordable prices. All Cass Art stores have simple, customer friendly layouts showcasing world-renowned manufacturers and provides a distinct and enjoyable retail experience for professionals, students and hobbyists alike.

ロンドン最大のアート関連商品を扱う専門店キャス・アート。高品質の画材を、手頃な価格で提供することをモットーとしています。店舗はすべて、シンプルで見やすいレイアウトで構成され、世界的に有名なメーカーの商品もラインナップ。プロから学生、趣味で利用する人まで満足させるユニークで楽しいショップです。

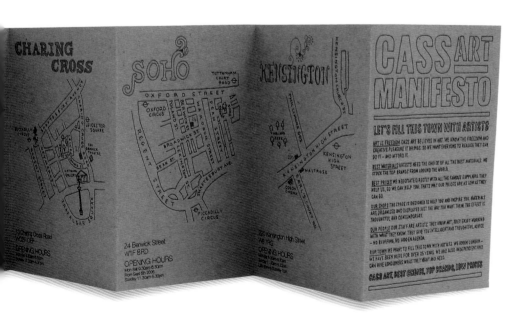

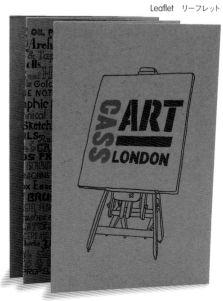

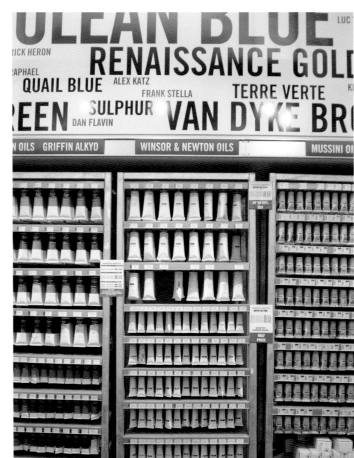

Books for Cooks

ブックス・フォー・クックス

Book

書店

▶ 4 Blenheim Crescent, London W11 1NN
http://www.booksforcooks.com

A, LD, Interior Design, Graphic Design:General Practice   CD:Eric Treuille   AD:Rosie Kindersley   P:Akiko Watanabe

Bookmark
しおり

Event Pamphlet
イベント案内

Notting Hill's famous cookbook shop, Books for Cooks is crammed with thousands of tasty titles and equipped with a squashy sofa for cookbook junkies in need of a long read. In this shop we really do cook the books – cookbooks are put to the test in our café at the back of the shop, while cookery classes take place in the demonstration kitchen upstairs.

ノッティングヒルにある有名な料理本専門店。店内には何千冊もの魅力的な本がところ狭しと並び、長居したい料理本ファンにはうれしい、柔らかなソファも用意されています。また、奥にあるカフェでは本のレシピが実際に試作され、2階のデモンストレーションキッチンでは料理教室が開催されるなど、料理も手がける書店です。

Kiehl's Since 1851 キール

CD:Victoria Maddocks

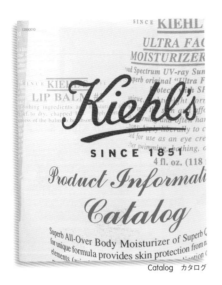

Post Card
ポストカード

Catalog　カタログ

Simple, no-frills packaging and a policy of not advertising allow Kiehl's to formulate its products with high quantities of the most efficacious ingredients available. In addition, Kiehl's has gained a reputation for generous sampling, with a "try before you buy" philosophy that has built a loyal fan base the world over through the word-of- mouth recommendations of its cherished customers.

シンプルで飾り気のないパッケージを使用し、宣伝をしないことで、厳選された原料をたっぷり使った商品展開が可能となっています。さらに「ご購入前にお試しください」という哲学に基づいて、惜しみなく試供品をくれることでも高く評価されています。そのうわさは口コミで広がり、世界中に根強いファンを獲得しました。

FOOD

The Butcher & Grill ブッチャー&グリル

Charcuttire, Bar and Grill　レストラン、精肉

39-41 Parkgate Road, Battersea, London
▶ SW11 4NP
http://www.thebutcherandgrill.com

A, CD, AD, LD, CW, Graphic Design, Interior Design:Dominic Ford　P:Kenichi Nakao

The Butcher & Grill is a combination of a modern butcher shop and a traditional British restaurant serving grilled meats as well as traditional British fare.

ブッチャー＆グリルは現代的な精肉店と昔ながらのブリティッシュ・レストランが融合したショップ。レストランでは、肉料理をはじめ、伝統的なイギリス料理を提供しています。

Shopping Bag
ショッピングバッグ

Menu
メニュー

Menu　メニュー

Shop Card　ショップカード

**THE
BUTCHER
& GRILL**

BAR & GRILL 020 7924 3999
BUTCHER SHOP 020 7924 3565
FAX 020 7223 7977
info@thebutcherandgrill.com
www.thebutcherandgrill.com

39 – 41 PARKGATE ROAD
BATTERSEA
LONDON SW11 4NP

nt Emilion   France
             Australia
elles Vignes' France
maine La   France
o 2003   Italy
e,   France
03
a Valley 2004 Australia
ago 2004   New Zealand
osme, 2004   France
rdot,   Spain
Fronsac 2002 France
maine des   France
2   Spain

RED WINES

88	Malbec, J Alberto, Patagonia 2004	Argentina	£42.50
89	Puerto Salinas Alicante, Bodegas Sierra, 2003	Spain	£45.00
90	Nuits St.Georges 1er Cru Les Damodes, Domaine Remoriquet 2000	France	£50.00
91	SC Pannell McLaren Vale Shiraz/Grenache 2004	Australia	£50.00
92	Les Tourelles de Lo... Pauillac 2002		£55.00
93	Amarone della Valp... Allegrini, 2001		
94	Chateau Pavie Mac... Grand Cru 1997		
95	Gevrey-Chambertin... 1er Cru, Sylvie Esm...		
96	Vega Sicilia 'Valbue... Duero 2000		
97	Domaine de Cheval...		
98	Chateau Pichon Lal...		

£7.25

BRISKET
RUMP
SHOULDER
TENDERLO
TOPSIDE
NECK

Wrapping Paper
ラッピングペーパー

Menu　メニュー

FISH AND VEGETARIAN	
£ 4.95	
£ 4.95	Fish of the day　Market Price
£ 5.50	Baked spinach and ricotta cannelloni　£11.50
£ 6.50	**SIDES**
£ 6.50	Bread and Butter　£ 1.50
£ 6.00	Chips　£ 2.75
£ 6.50	Mash　£ 2.75
	New potatoes　£ 2.75
£ 7.50	Dauphinoise potatoes　£ 2.75
£ 8.50	Steamed broccoli　£ 2.75
£ 9.50	Fried onions　£ 2.75
	Mixed leaf salad　£ 3.00
	Buttered spinach　£ 3.00
230g/8oz £ 8.50	Rocket and Parmesan salad　£ 4.00
230g/8oz £ 8.50	Grilled mushrooms with garlic　£ 2.75
700g/25oz £45.00	Endive with mustard dressing　£ 3.00
230g/8oz £ 9.50	**STUFF ON THE SIDE**
280g/10oz £12.50	Béarnaise　Free
280g/10oz £13.50	Green peppercorn sauce　Free
230g/8oz £15.00	Red wine sauce　Free
280g/10oz £ 9.50	Hollandaise　Free
x1 £ 6.00	Aïoli　Free
x1 £10.00	Onion gravy　Free
400g/14oz £12.50	Garlic and parsley butter　Free
230g/8oz £11.50	Salsa verde　Free
450g/16oz £18.50	Caper and lemon sauce　Free
£13.50	Honey, soy and sesame　Free
£13.50	
£ 6.50	**DESSERTS**
	Lemon meringue pie served with cream　£ 5.00
£13.50	Chocolate fondant with Chantilly cream　£ 5.00
	Apple crumble with vanilla ice cream　£ 5.00
£12.50	Panna Cotta, pineapple and peppercorn compote, coconut cookie　£ 5.00
£14.50	Selection of cheese, pickles and chutneys　£ 7.50
£12.50	Selection ice creams and sorbets　£ 5.00
£13.50	
	KIDS MENU (2 courses)　£5.25

dough with shallot and

potatoes, wild mushrooms, vinaigrette

vinegar

from the counter
...ets
...hop
...ope
...t
...d calf's liver with mash, parsley and tomato
...free range chicken

...ED
...ef in Battersea Power Porter beer, with horseradish
...e dumplings
...lder braised with prunes, Guinness, black pepper and sage
...n with creamed polenta
... Lamb's offal with onions and Portobello mushrooms
...ll pineapple glazed duck breast with braised Puy lentil

Chipolata sausages with mash and Heinz baked beans
Pasta with grated Cheddar, Parmesan and butter
Grilled cheese and ham on toast with loads of ketchup
Breaded Plaice fillet with chips and green beans
Mini roast of the day (Sundays only)

Ice cream with chocolate sauce
Fresh fruit

Port
Quinta de la Rosa LBV　£5.00
...ailado　£7.50
...tawny
...maraens　£8.50

...magnac & More...
...rie, Selection,　£5.50
...rie, ...eserve, Cognac　£7.50
...castaing, Armagnac　£5.50
...KO Armagnac　£7.00
...e, VSOP Calvados　£5.00
...e, 15 year old　£6.50
...e, ... Roque　6.00
... Capri Natura　£4.50
...ck Unicum　£5.00
...chiata, Pilzer　£5.50
...iava, Pilzer　£6.00

£2.25

...ur waiter)

...ast

	£2.40
	£1.85
	£1.85
	£2.50
...so	£2.30
	£2.40
	£2.00
	£2.50
	£2.50

Soft Drinks/Water
Lorina Pink Lemonade
Firefly "Wake Up" Peach & Green tea
Firefly "Chill Out" Blackcurrant, Redcurrant & Cinnamon
Firefly "Detox" Lemon, Lime & Ginger
Chegworth Valley, Cox & Bramley Apple Juice
Fresh Orange Juice
Juices
Coca Cola Bottles
Diet Coca Cola
Milkshakes
Coke Float
Red Bull
Belu, fizzy water 330ml
Belu still water, 330ml
Belu, fizzy water 750ml
Belu still water, 750ml

Minerals/Mixers
Bitter Lemon
Soda
Tonic Water
Slim Line Tonic Water
Ginger Ale
Lemonade

Brompton Quarter Café

ブロンプトン・クォーター・カフェ

Restaurant, Cafe, Bakery and Events
レストラン、カフェ、ベーカリー、イベント
223-225 Brompton Road, Knightsbridge,
London SW3 2EJ
http://www.bromptonquartercafe.com

A, CD, Interior Design:Maria Mallalieu   LD, Graphic Design:Rashna Mody-Clark   P:Kenichi Nakao

Brompton Quarter is all about being a food emporium with a slant towards the rich food of the Mediterranean. Everything is made fresh in house and with the best ingredients including all organic meat. The main decorative features are the mirrored wall by Robert Pratt McMachan and the drippy chandeliers by Piet Boon Zone.

地中海の豊潤な食品を中心に扱う大規模食料品店。100％オーガニックミートをはじめ、最高の材料だけを使用して、すべて店内で調理された出来たての惣菜たちが並んでいます。ロバート・プラット・マクマカンによる鏡張りの壁とピエト・ブーン・ゾーンによる、たわわなシャンデリアが目を惹きます。

Bread

	75p
Petit Pain	90p
Mini Baguette	£1.50
Baguette 280g	£1.50
Pain Sportif 150g	£3.90
Pain Sportif 500g	£3.25
Pain Complet 500g	£3.25
Pain Paysan	£3.25
Pain de Compagne 500g (Grain)	£3.25
Pain au Levain 500g (White)	£5.25
Pain au Levain 1kg (White)	£3.25
Pain au Levain 500g (Wholemeal)	£5.25
Pain au Levain 1kg (Wholemeal)	£3.25
Challa 500g	£3.25
Ciabatta Italiane 500g	£1.00
Ciabatta Italiane Small	£3.25
Le Pain de Mie	£3.45
Foccacia 500g	£1.50
Foccacia Small Square	£3.25
Pain de Seigle 500g	£3.50
Le Pain de Cartage 500g	£3.90
Walnut Bread 500g	

Food To Go

Epicerie Fine
Traiteur-Boulanger-Patissier

Breakfast Menu

Fruit Salad & yogurt	£4.50
Granola & yogurt	£4.95
Granola with fruit & yogurt	£5.95

Gourmet Bar Menu

Hot / 2

Smoked Haddock & Salon Fish Cakes	£9.75
Marinated Grilled Calamari	£9.75
Organic Lamb Casserole	£10.25
Organic Beef Stroginoff	£10.25
Organic Baked Salmon	£10.25
Organic Beef Bourguignon	£11.25
Roasted Organic Butterfly Turkey Breast	£11.25

Hot Drinks Menu

Hot Drinks

Cappuccino	£1.95
Latte	£1.95
Double Espresso	£1.95
Espresso	£1.50
Black Coffee	£1.95
Hot Chocolate	£2.20
Mocа	£2.20
Tea	
Earl Grey	£1.50
English Breakfast	£1.50
Camomile	£1.50
Green	£1.50
Fennel	£1.50
Peppermint	£1.50
Verven	£1.50
Fresh Mint Tea	£1.95

Brompton Quarter Café prides itself on a Patisserie range that is too big to list! Please look at our cake counter to see our daily delights.

Opening Hours

Mon-Fri 7.30am to 11pm

Sat-Sun 8am to 11pm

Tel: 020 7225 2107

Fax: 020 7225 2108

Menu メニュー

The Hummingbird Bakery

ハミングバード・ベーカリー

Home-Baking　お菓子

▶ 133 Portobello Road, Notting Hill, London
W11 2DY
http://www.hummingbirdbakery.com

A, Interior Design:Jason Milne & Sue Wheldon, Brandarchitects UK   CD, AD:Sue Wheldon, Brandarchitects, UK
LD, Graphic Design:Sue Thedens, Brandarchitects, UK   P:Akiko Watanabe

In designing The Hummingbird Bakery, we wanted to recreate a homey, warm, old-fashioned American kitchen feeling.   We used colours that mimic our dark chocolate and bubble gum pink cupcakes!   Our service is relaxed and friendly and puts our customers at ease when choosing their perfect cake.

ハミングバード・ベーカリーの店舗を設計する際、意識したのは家庭的で温かい昔ながらのアメリカンキッチン。店内に採用した配色は、ベーカリーが販売するダークチョコとバブルガムピンクのカップケーキの色です。お客様が気楽にケーキを選ぶことができるように、リラックスしたフレンドリーな応対をしています。

Tea Smith ティー・スミス

Tea and Teaware
紅茶、紅茶用品
▶ 6 Lamb Street, Spitalfields, London E1 6EA
http://www.teasmith.co.uk

A, Interior design:Jonathan Clark Architects   CD:Tomoko Kawase   AD, LD, Graphic Design:Rashna Mody-Clark
P:Kenichi Nakao

Tea Smith is the place where the 'Nation of Tea Drinkers' can rediscover the aromas and tastes of the world's best teas. The authentic materials and design, evokes Japanese and Chinese elements, while being at home in the heart of Spitalfields, London's most vibrant location for independent retailers.

「紅茶の国」の人々が、世界各地から集められた選りすぐりのお茶の香りとおいしさを再発見できる場となっているティースミス。店内に置かれた本格的な茶道具やデザインが、日本や中国を思わせます。個人リテイラーの集まる活気溢れるスピタルフィールズの中心に位置する、親しみやすい雰囲気のショップです。

Package
パッケージ

Letterhead　レターヘッド

Shop Card　ショップカード

Rococo Chocolates

ロココ・チョコレート ▶

Confectionery
チョコレート菓子
321 king's Road, London SW3 5EP
http://www.rococochocolates.com/

Interior Design:Mark Priceman   LD:Chantal Coady   Graphic Design:Patrick Simon (for 2006 catalog, supervised by Chantal Coady)   CD:Chantal Coady   CW:Chantal Coady and James Booth   P:Yuki Sugiura

The serious study of Chocolate is infused into the presentation of the company. The adventure of scholarship implies the innovation and quality of the company. Blending the sharp geometry of the Mayas and Aztecs with an European collector's taste for presenting the exotic, the shop interiors evoke the pleasures of the 'curiosity cabinet'.

チョコレートを本格的に研究し商品開発を行っているショコラテリー。あくなき研究心はこの企業の革新性と高品質を物語っています。マヤ、アステカ文明のシャープな幾何学模様とヨーロッパのコレクターの異国趣味を融合させたショップのインテリアは、宝物がたくさん詰まったキャビネットを彷彿させます。

Catalog　カタログ

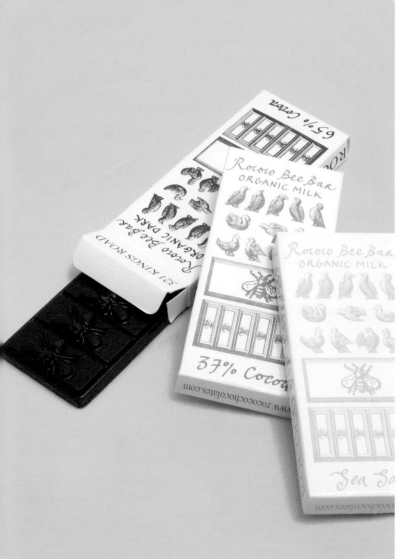

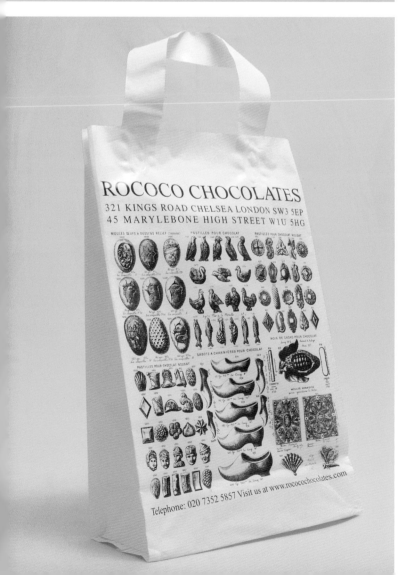

Yauatcha ヤウアチャ

Restaurant, Tea House & Retail
レストラン、ティールーム、菓子販売
▶ 15 Broadwick Street, London W1F

A, Interior Design:Christian Liaigre CD, AD:Alan Yau D:Made Thought P:Kenichi Nakao

Yauatcha is an all day dim-sum restaurant & tea house, owned by restaurateur Alan Yau. It has a wide array of teas from Asia and tea related products inspired by the tea list.

ヤウアチャは1日じゅう点心が楽しめるレストラン＆ティーハウス。レストラン経営者アラン・ヤウがオーナーを務めるこのレストランでは、アジアから取り寄せたバラエティ豊かなお茶の数々が楽しめます。また、これらのティーリストに着想を得て制作されたお茶にまつわる商品も扱っています。

Tea House
Patisserie & Tea List

Menu メニュー

YAUATCHA
丘記茶苑

Citrus Rice Queen

Catalog カタログ

Hakkasan ハッカサン

Interior Design:Christian Liaigre LD, Graphic Design:North P:Kenich Nakao

Menu
メニュー

Cloakroom Number
クローク番号

Hidden in the basement level of a quiet back street off Oxford street, Hakkasan is a classy Chinese restaurant owned by the well-known restauranteur, Alan Yau, the man behind Yauatcha and Busaba. The slick and elegant interior was designed by Christian Liaigre and features an oriental touch in the details. A space that is removed from reality combined with innovative food and cocktails all create a special experience at Hakkasan.

オックスフォードst.近くの静かな路地の地下にひっそりたたずむハッカサンは、ヤウアチャやブッサバのオーナーとして有名なアラン・ヤウが経営する高級中華料理店。気品あふれる店内はクリスチャン・リアーグルによるもので、オリエンタルな雰囲気。非日常的な空間と斬新な食事やカクテルが、特別な空間を演出します。

The Bombay Bicycle Club

ボンベイ・バイシクル・クラブ

CD:Tracey Kitchener-Kemp   P:Akiko Watanabe

Takeaway Box
テイクアウト用ボックス

Welcome to The Bombay Bicycle Club

The Bombay Bicycle Club was a popular gathering place in the Northern part of the Indian sub-continent, where the first colonial officers and soldiers used to gather during the time of the Raj. Food and refreshments were served as visitors relaxed and caught up on the events of the day.

Indian cuisine has evolved dramatically over the past centuries from the most basic of foods into the varied and exciting dishes that we see today. Many cultures have influenced this development including the Chinese use of spices and the traditional Mongolian hot pot cooking.

Arguably one of the most important influences came from the Persian invaders, who established the Mughal Empire and ruled for several hundred years. During their reign they built the Taj Mahal and many other well known monuments. For our part, the greatest contribution was their culinary expertise. The daal and rice of the early civilisation remained but added to this were a variety of spices such as Saffron and Garam Masala. Soon after, the Tandoor clay oven was introduced as a means of cooking the marinated meat and leavened bread called the naan. Even the idea of concluding a meal with sweets came from the Persians.

It is this philosophy of creating simple, yet fresh and inventive Indian food, using raw ingredients of the highest quality that is fundamental to The Bombay Bicycle Club today. Our menu is designed to suit the taste of the European palate; spicy and aromatic but not searing hot. Our chef will be pleased to prepare your meal to your specific taste.

The Restaurants

The Bombay Bicycle Club restaurant opened in Nightingale Lane, Clapham twenty years ago. It is widely acknowledged by many of London's top chefs and restaurant critics as the benchmark for fresh Indian cooking within local communities.

The Bombay Bicycle Club restaurants have become the destination for seekers of quality Indian food which is served by friendly and airy atmosphere, with floral displays.

To make a reservation for Nightingale Lane, call 020 8673 6217.

To make a reservation for Hampstead, call 020 7435 3544

To make a reservation for Holland Park, call 020 7727 7335

The Party Catering Service

Due to popular demand, The Bombay Bicycle Club has introduced a catering service. We would be delighted to discuss your party plans for anything from twenty up to four hundred guests. Everything can be tailored to suit your specific requirements to make sure the event is a great success.

As always, our Chefs will cook your favourite Bombay Bicycle Club dishes to order. We are also able to supply staff, cutlery, glassware and crockery. For further information please call our office and ask to speak with Olly.

Our Service

At the Bombay Bicycle Club we aim to provide our customers with the very best levels of exceptional service. We are constantly trying to improve your experience and would welcome any feedback that you may have to help us do so. Please call our Managing Director, on 020 7071 8430 or email her at sarahw@thebombaybicycleclub.com

Your Nearest Kitchen is:

ISLINGTON KITCHEN
020 7424 5353

Essex Road Islington
412 Essex Road
Islington
London
020 7424 5353

(We reserve the right to exclude certain areas)

Open Monday to Saturday 6.00pm - 11.00pm
Sunday 6.00pm - 10.30pm

www.thebombaybicycleclub.com

FREE delivery on orders over £7.00 - or a £2.00 charge will be applied. If you have any problems or queries please do not hesitate to call. Our staff are there to help you. PAYMENT By credit card, with telephone order or on collection. By cheque, supported by valid cheque card, on delivery or on collection. By cash On delivery or on collection.

The Bombay Bicycle Club...   ...only tell your best

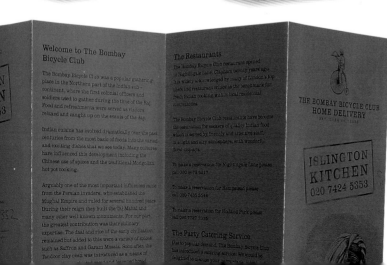

Leaflet
リーフレット

The Bombay Bicycle Club was a stylish gathering place on the Indian sub-continent where colonial officers would take trips, country picnics always with delicious food. The first Bombay Bicycle Club Restaurant opened 20 years ago and the first stand-alone kitchen opened in 1995. All of our restaurant's qualities have simply been transferred to these kitchens where we provide the finest quality food.

植民地時代、役人たちが訪れ食事を楽しんだインドのお洒落な人気スポット「ザ・ボンベイ・クラブ」が名前の由来。当レストランの1号店がオープンしたのは20年前で、1995年からは独立したデリバリーキッチンを展開。レストランのクオリティがそのままデリバリーキッチンに受け継がれ、最高の料理を提供しています。

Shop Card　ショップカード

Menu　メニュー

Poilane ポワラーヌ

A, CD, AD, D, LD, I, CW, Interior Design:Lionel Poilane   P:Akiko Watanabe

Shop Card　ショップカード

Leaflet
リーフレット

Poilane, a French bakery famous for its sourdough bread, has it's first London shop in Belgravia. Founded in 1932 by Pierre Poilane and expanded in the 70's by his son Lionel Poilane is currently directed by his daugher Apollonia Poilane. The shop is simple, charming and intimate. The bread is freshly baked every day on the premises.

サワードウのパンが有名なフレンチベーカリー、ポワラーヌのロンドン1号店はベルグレイビアにあります。1932年にピエール・ポワラーヌが創業し、70年代に息子のリオネルが拡張。現在店を取り仕切るのはその娘のアポロニアです。シンプルで魅力的な店舗はくつろいだ雰囲気。パンは毎日、店内で焼き上げています。

Gift Box
ギフトボックス

Konditor & Cook

コンディトール＆クック

D:Colin Melia　Interior Design:Azman Owens Architects　P:Akiko Watanabe

Bespoke Bakery and Food

洋菓子、食品

▶ 46 Grays Inn Road, London WC1X 8LR
http://www.konditorandcook.com

Konditor & Cook is celebrated for it's contemporary approach to cake decorating and commitment to quality. This approach is carried through to the presentation of the food, as well as the retail environment, where contemporary architecture & stylish packaging enhance the customers' experience.

ケーキのデコレーションに対する新しいアプローチや品質へのこだわりで名高いコンディトール＆クック。そのアプローチは、フードの見せ方や店づくりにも一貫して受け継がれています。現代的な建物とスタイリッシュなパッケージが、コンディトール＆クックの魅力をよりいっそう高めています。

Gift Box
ギフトボックス

Rivington Bar & Grill

リビングトン バー＆グリル

CD:Mark Hix　P:Kenich Nakao

Restaurant and Bar

レストラン、バー

▶ 28-30 Rivington Street, London EC2A 3DZ
http://www.rivingtongrill.co.uk

Located in the heart of Shoreditch, home to many art galleries, Rivington Shoreditch displays neon-art piece by Tim Noble and Sue Webster and neon work by Peter Saville. Our ingredients are sourced from small suppliers in and around the British Isles, harvesting responsibly from ocean and sea-shore, forest and farm. This fantastic local produce has provided the inspiration for many new recipes and is the focus of our seasonally-changing menu.

ギャラリーの多いショーディッチ地区の中心に位置するこの店にはティム・ノーブルやスー・ウェブスター、ピーター・サヴィルのネオン作品が飾られています。近隣の小規模な業者から仕入れた選りすぐりの食材を使用。地産のすばらしい食材は多くの新しいレシピを生み出し、季節ごとに変わるメニューの目玉となっています。

ASSOCIATES	STEL
DICKSMITH	DUNCAN
COUNTER	TATIANA ECHEVERRI
WHITECHAPEL	BELLME & K
MAUREEN PALEY	GILLIAM
APPROACH	JOHN
MODERN ART	MONAHA
WHITE CUBE	CAROLL
CHISENHALE	BE
FORTESCUE AVE	EMILY
KATE MACGARRY	
HOTEL	RICHA
STORE	
FLOWERS EAST	ROBERT
AGENCY	
TROLLEY	
FOSTER	BIANCA
MUSEUM 52	
DAVID RISLEY	JONATHAN W
THE RELIANCE	
FRED	SIMO
BISCHOFF/WEISS	TATIAN
HAUSER & WIRTH	CRISTOP
MADDER ROSE	VANISH

Fish Works
フィッシュ・ワークス

CD:Mitch Tonks P:Akiko Watanabe

Sea Food Restaurant and Fish Mongul
シーフードレストラン、魚屋

▶ 188 Westbourne Grove, London W11 2RH
http://www.fishworks.co.uk

Owned by the restaurateur, food writer and chef, Mitch Tonks, Fish Works is all about eating, buying and enjoying fabulous seafood. There are now several FishWorks venues spread across the south of England, including our award-winning restaurants in Bath, Marylebone and Chiswick. We run cookery schools and also have a successful home delivery service offering fresh fish, prepared to customers' requirements, delivered overnight from Brixham to their door.

レストラン経営者、フードライター、シェフの顔をもつミッチ・トンクスの店。魚介類の販売も行うおいしいシーフードレストラン。受賞歴をもつバース、メリルボン、チズィックの店など英国南部に数店舗をもち、料理教室も開講。要望に合わせて、新鮮な魚をブリクサムの漁港から翌日配達してくれる宅配サービスも好評です。

Wrapping Paper
ラッピングペーパー

Suburb

サバーブ

Art, Music, Coffee and Juice Bar
アート、音楽、コーヒー、ジュースバー
▶ 19 Shorts Gardens, Neal's Yard, Covent Garden, London WC2H 9AW
http://www.suburbstore.com

Interior Design:Mark Ingham   CD:James Henry   Graphic Design:Robin Powell   P:Akiko Watanabe

Setting out to create a unique experience in the world of corporate chain stores, a test between a creative concept of art/music/coffee and juice bar and building a successful business, .. join the world of suburb at suburbstore.com

チェーン展開するショップという枠組みの中で、ユニークな体験をつくりだそうと生まれたサバーブ。アート、音楽、コーヒー＆ジュースバーとして独創的なコンセプトを打ち出しつつ、ビジネスとして成功させようという試みです。ショップのウェブサイトsuburbstore.comにて、一度サバーブの世界を覗いてみては？

La Fromagerie ラ・フロマジェリー

CD:Patricia Michelson　P:Kenichi Nakao

Cheese, Dairy Shop and Cafe
チーズ、食品、カフェ
▶ 2-4 Moxon Street, Marylebone, London W1U 4EW
http://www.lafromagerie.co.uk/

Sticker
ステッカー

Patricia Michelson's award winning shop stocks nearly 200 varieties of fine cheeses, which are kept separately in a fragrant room, as well as wines, meats, fruit, and bread from Poilane. There is a dining table at the back of the shop where customers can enjoy daily-changing menu of soups, salads and savoury tarts.

パトリシア・マイケルソンによる、受賞歴をもつこのショップでは、別室（フレグラント・ルーム）に保存された約200種類の良質なチーズをはじめ、ワイン、肉、果物、ポワラーヌのパンを提供しています。店の奥にはダイニングテーブルがしつらえられ、日替わりのスープやサラダ、惣菜系タルトなどを楽しむことができます。

Letterhead　レターヘッド

Menu　メニュー

Sticker　ステッカー

Gift Box
ギフトボックス

Itsu (Bishops Gate) イツ

CD, AD, LD, Interior Design, Packaging Design:Afroditikrassa Ltd   P:Akiko Watanabe

Restaurant   レストラン

10-11 Broadgate Arcade, 155 Bishopsgate
London EC2M 3TQ
http://www.itsu.com

A new concept Sushi & salad restaurant, Itsu supplies healthy, tasty and affordable food. A variety of sushi rolls, sashimi, dumplings and salads are served in beautifully designed packaging. Bold graphics and pop colours which accompany the Itsu logo are seen consistently through packaging, the interior displays and seating areas.

新しいコンセプトの寿司＆サラダ・レストランは、ヘルシーでおいしくて、値段もお手頃。寿司ロールや刺身、餃子やシューマイ、サラダなど、種類豊富な料理が美しくデザインされたパッケージで供されます。パッケージ、インテリアディスプレイ、客席には大胆なグラフィックとポップな色使い、イツのロゴが採用されています。

Primrose Bakery

プリムローズ・ベーカリー

LD:Michael Heath　P:Kenichi Nakao

Cake
ケーキ

▶ 69 Gloucester Ave, London NW1 8LD
http://www.primrosebakery.org.uk/

Founded in 2004, Primrose Bakery started out baking for children's parties but we quickly noticed how well the cupcakes went down with adults! We have tried to keep it to simple, old-fashioned cooking, using good quality ingredients, such as organic eggs, fresh milk and butter – ingredients you might use at home when baking for your own children, friends and family.

2004年オープン当初は、子どものパーティー向けのベーカリーとしてスタートしたプリムローズ。ここのカップケーキはたちまち大人たちの間でも評判に。オーガニック卵、新鮮な牛乳やバターなど、家庭で子どもや友人や家族のためにパンを焼くとき選ぶような良質な材料を使い、昔ながらのシンプルな製法で焼いています。

Shop Card　ショップカード

The Cinnamon Club

シナモン・クラブ ▶

A, CD, AD, D, LD:In-house   P:Kenichi Nakao

Restaurant   レストラン

The Old Westminster Library, 30-32 Great
Smith Street, London SW1P 3BU
http://www.cinnamonclub.com

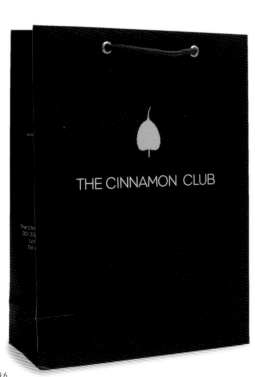

Letterhead　レターヘッド

Set in the beautiful Grade II listed Old Westminster Library, The Cinnamon Club has revolutionised Indian cuisine in the UK. The award-winning restaurant serves Modern Indian dishes designed to reflect the culinary traditions and depths of the sub-continent. Complete with private dining room, mezzanine area, library bar and subterranean bar, The Cinnamon Club is one of London's favourite fine dining destinations.

歴史建造物グレードⅡに指定されているオールド・ウェストミンスター・ライブラリー内にある、英国インド料理界に革命を起こした名店。受賞歴をもち、本場インドの伝統的で奥深い料理法を取り入れた現代インド料理を提供します。個室や中二階スペース、ライブラリーバーや地下のバーを備えた、ロンドン屈指の人気店です。

Aubaine オーベイン

Restaurant and Bakery
レストラン、ベーカリー
▶ 262 Brompton Road, London SW3 2AS
http://www.aubaine.co.uk

Interior Design:Franck Andrew CD:Hani Nakkash CW:Aubaine I, LD:FLO Bailey P:Kenichi Nakao

Sticker
ステッカー

Aubaine Restaurant, Boulangerie and Patisserie is a sophisticated yet relaxed establishment that serves traditional French meals, freshly baked breads and delicious patisserie. Located in the fashionable and cultural heart of London, Aubaine has become a popular place to visit for local residents and tourists alike. The room is light and airy, decorated with jars of homemade jams and carefully crafted cakes and macaroons.

レストラン、ブランジェリー、パティスリーを併設するオーベインは洗練されつつも、くつろげる空間。正統派フレンチや焼き立てパン、おいしいケーキを提供しています。ファッションと文化の中心地あり、地元民や観光客に人気のスポットです。明るく開放的な室内には、自家製ジャムや美しいケーキ、マカロンが飾られています。

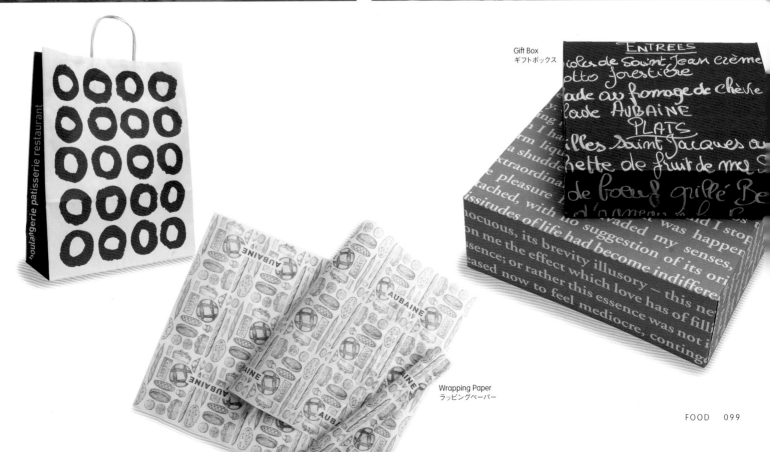

Gift Box
ギフトボックス

Wrapping Paper
ラッピングペーパー

Peyton & Byrne ペイトン&バーン

A, Interior Design:FAT   LD, Graphic Design:Farrow Design

Bakery　ベーカリー

The Heal's Building, 196 Tottenham Court
Road, London W1T 7LQ
http://www.peytonandbyrne.co.uk

The new Peyton & Byrne Bakery by Oliver Peyton is British traditional baking at its best. It will include fabulous cakes, pastries, breads and savouries, handmade each day by Roger Pizey, one of Britain's leading pastry chefs. Peyton & Byrne's own range of special teas and coffees is available to take away.

伝統的なパンや焼き菓子を最高のクオリティで提供する、オリバー・ペイトンがプロデュースする新しいベーカリーです。英国屈指のペイストリーシェフ、ロジャー・パイゼイが、ケーキ、ペイストリー、パン、オーブン料理を毎日焼き上げます。バラエティに富んだスペシャル・ティーやコーヒーはテイクアウトで。

PEYTON AND BYRNE

Opening at Heal's
A British bakery

...ductory Gift

...complimentary bag of Peyton and Byrne loose leaf
...ea when purchasing a large boxed cake *

...Byrne cakes, breads and savouries are handmade each
...Pizey, one of Britain's leading pastry chefs.

...d cakes including a time-honoured Victoria sponge,
...kewell tart and an indulgent chocolate layered cake
...el coloured pastries and homemade biscuits.

...e tarts, terrines and pies such as pork or steak
...fillings like rare roast beef with classic
...freshly prepared sandwiches with classic
...Lancashire cheese with creamed horseradish or crumbly
...with piccalilli.

Peyton and Byrne also produce their own range of teas, coffees,
preserves and confectionary, all made using only the highest
quality ingredients and beautifully packaged.

Peyton and Byrne,
The Heal's Building, 196 Tottenham Court Road, London W1
020 7580 2522
peytonandbyrne.com

Opening Times:
Monday – Wednesday 8.00am – 6.00pm
Thursday 8.00am – 8.00pm
Friday 8.00am – 6.30pm
Saturday 9.30am – 6.00pm
Sunday 12.00 – 6.00...

Melrose and Morgan

メルローズ＆モルガン

A, Interior Design:Mike Deely, Ian James　LD, Graphic Design:Kerr Noble　P:Kenich Nakao

Grocery

食料雑貨

▶　42 Gloucester Avenue, London NW1 8JD
http://www.melroseandmorgan.com

Melrose and Morgan takes you away from the supermarket and brings back personal grocery shopping. Helpful, knowledgeable assistants shop with the customer, informing them about the predominately British seasonal products available. At the heart of the shop is a 'live' kitchen where customers watch pies, tarts, stews and soups being prepared. The customer sees the whole process and can ask the chefs questions and advice.

一度ここで買い物をすると、もうスーパーには行けません。親切で知識豊富なスタッフが、旬の食材などの商品情報を提供しながら買い物をサポートしてくれるのです。店の中心にはライブキッチンがあり、パイやタルト、シチュー、スープなどの調理工程を見ることができ、シェフに質問したりアドバイスをもらったりもできます。

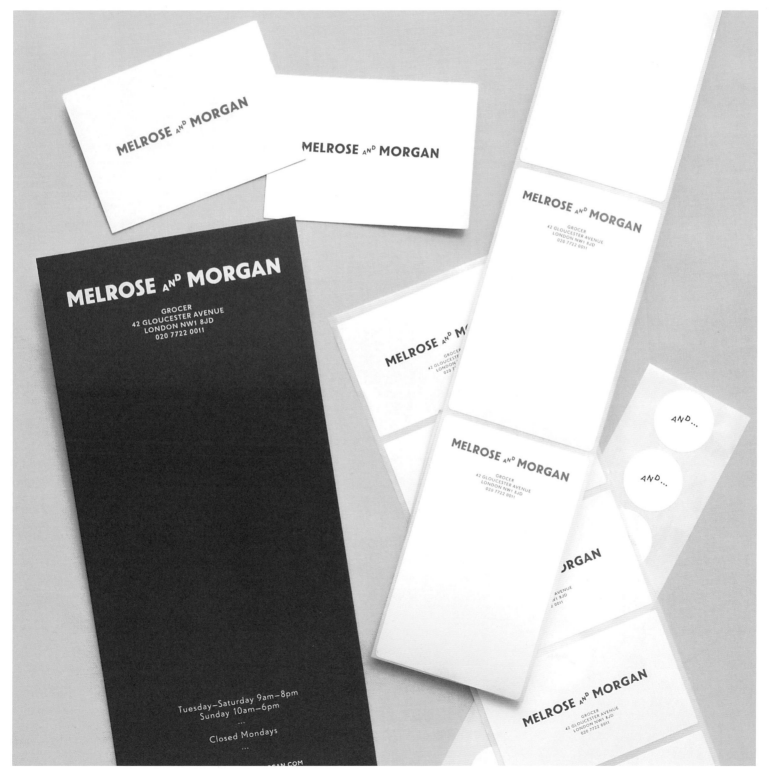

Ping Pong ピンポン

Restaurant　レストラン

▶ 45 Great Marlborough Street, Soho, London
W1F 7JL
http://www.pingpongdimsum.com

AD, D, LD:Niclas Sellebraten　A:David Marquardt (MACH Architektur)　P:Kenichi Nakao

Our philosophy is to create a venue that blends contemporary style with an authentic Chinese aesthetic. Then provide a fantastic shared dining experience, traditional dim sum of the very highest quality - prepared to the most exacting standards, and exceptional customer service.

現代的なスタイルと中国の伝統美を融合した空間をつくり出すことが、このレストランのこだわりです。その空間が、すばらしい食事を楽しめる場となっています。ピンポンでは、最高級の伝統的な点心が、実に手の込んだレシピにのっって調理され、とびきりのサービスとともに提供されます。

ping pong

Baked puffs £2.99 each	....Roast pork ....Chicken ....Vegetable v
Steamed dishes £2.99 each	....Chicken feet ....Squid in satay sauce
Steamed dumplings £2.99 each	....Chive ....Har gau (prawn & bamboo) ....Coriander ....Crystal v ....Scallop & shiitake ....Pork shu mai ....Spring onion & coriander wonton ....Shanghai siew long bun ....Seafood ....Spinach & mushroom v ....Spicy pork ....Spicy vegetable v ....Snow pea & mushroom ....Spicy chicken
Steamed rolls £2.99 each	....Chinese leaf wrap ....Spinach prawn wrap ....Vegetarian bean curd v
Steamed buns £2.99 each	....Char sui bun ....Chicken bun ....Vegetable bun v
Fried rolls £2.99 each	....Crispy hoi sin duck roll ....Vietnamese spring roll ....Vegetable spring roll v ....Jasmine chicken ....Crispy Thai chicken
Fried delicacies £2.99 each	....Crispy prawn ball ....Prawn toast ....Vegetable layer dumpling v ....Chilli squid cake ....Spinach & pork wonton ....Prawn & garlic bean curd wrap
Sticky rice £3.10 each	....Traditional ....Vegetarian v ....Seafood ....Honey glazed ribs

Vegetables
£2.99
	....Choy sum in soy sauce topp...
	    with fried garlic
	....Steamed broccoli in
	    spicy garlic sauce
	....Selection of pickled veg...

Set menu	....Seafood lunch ....Vegetarian lunch v ....Mixed lunch ....Dumpling fix
Ice-cream (3 scoops)	....Choice of flavour...

Menu
メニュー

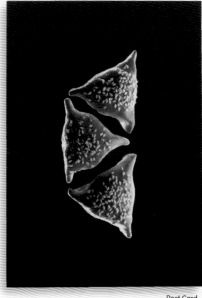

Ping Pong Dim Sum 點心
Little steamed parcels of deliciousness

ping pong

45 Great Marlborough Street, London W1F 7JL
T +44 (0)20 7851 6969   Fax: +44 (0)20 7851 6968

74-76 Westbourne Grove, London W2 5SH
T +44 (0)20 7313 9832   Fax: +44 (0)20 7313 9849

10 Paddington Street, London W1U 5QL
T +44 (0)20 7009 9600   Fax: +44 (0)20 7009 9601

29a James Street, London W1U 1DZ
T +44 (0)20 7034 3100   Fax: +44 (0)20 7034 3101

48 Eastcastle Street, London W1W 8DX
Tel +44 (0)20 7079 0550   Fax: +44 (0)20 7079 0557

48 Newman Street, London W1T 1QQ
Tel +44 (0)20 7291 3080   Fax: +44 (0)20 7291 3082

www.pingpongdimsum.com

Shop Card   ショップカード

Post Card
ポストカード

ping pong

Carluccio's Caffé

カルルッチオズ・カフェ

Interior Design:Design LSM

Cafe, Deli and Food　カフェ、デリ、食料品

▶ Westbourne Corner, 108 Westbourne Grove,
London W2 5RU
http://www.carluccios.com

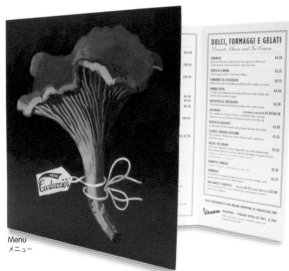

Menu
メニュー

Leaflet　リーフレット

Christmas Leaflet
クリスマス・リーフレット

Carluccio's Christmas Menu 2006

CONTENTS

A MERRY CHRISTMAS TO YOU ALL and a hearty welcome to this, our first and very special Carluccio's magazine. This year, we not only suggest festive touches and ideas to add Christmas magic to your home, but also bring the warmth of seasonal cooking to your table with Antonio's delicious and easy to make fireside suppers in Christmas with Carluccio's (P.4): simple food and ideas that are perfect for a family get-together around a glass of mulled wine. A warm mug of cocoa, a candle and snug blanket is all you need when you read Priscilla Carluccio's bed time story (P.10): Pinocchio and the Chocolate House.

Storytelling is a folk art in the Tuscan countryside, and has been for centuries. Priscilla at last allows Pinocchio good times, for he gets to lick the chocolate house. And we travel up high in to the snow-dusted mountains with Antonio, to taste Christmas in Friuli (P.12), a remote region in the north of Italy where the fairy tale charm of snow on Alpine cabin and forests, moody and dark, complete the picture-book magic of this our first Christmas magazine. His Friuli recipe for Jote Triestina, bean and sauerkraut soup, is one of those delicious slow pots of comforting, you'll be coming back for seconds and thirds.

Salute! Buone Feste!

Buon Appetito
From us all at Carluccio's

CHRISTMAS WITH CARLUCCIO'S

...endy drops in on Antonio & Priscilla Carluccio, ...eady for Christmas in the depths of the countryside.

Christmas is about fun', Priscilla says, stringing up a line of little moose-shaped fire lighters across her brick fireplace. She's perfectly right. 'It should not be about enormous stressful shopping trips,' Antonio appears from the wood attached to a wheelbarrow piled high with pumpkins and kindling twigs. 'I never said it wasn't about work', Priscilla adds. 'Everyone should join in. Chopping, stirring, washing up and putting away – but always with a glass of something good in hand.'

Insalata *di* Rinforzo
TOP-UP SALAD

Zuppa *di* Zucca e Porcini
PUMPKIN & C.E.P SOUP

Risotto *di* Zucca
PUMPKIN RISOTTO

Crostini *di* Funghi WILD MUSHROOM TOASTS

With their fabulous combination of contemporary Italian caffé, alimentary food shop and deli, Carluccio's caffés offers offer a genuine Italian tasting experience in a striking and modern environment.

現代的なイタリアンカフェと栄養たっぷりのフード・ショップ＆デリというすばらしいコンビネーションが売りのカルルッチオズ・カフェ。このカフェでは、印象的でモダンな空間の中、本格的なイタリアの味を体験することができます。

Mia Rigo ミア・リーゴ

CD, AD:Mia Rigo   Graphic Design:Andrew Roberts   P:Akiko Watanabe

Cafe
カフェ

▶ 14 Gloucester Road, London SW7 4RB
http://www.miarigo.com

Leaflet
リーフレット

Leaflet
リーフレット

Shop Card   ショップカード

Mia Rigo is a caffé for those that wish to experiment and linger! Caffé Karalis is our exclusive house coffee, Arabica in style, made since 1936 by a company who has resisted the temptation to mass produce. We also serve panini from all 19 regions of Italy. Mia Rigo is a local supplier of Italian foods you will want everyday.

新しいことを試しつつ、まったりした時間を過ごしたい人にぴったりのカフェ。ハウスコーヒー「カフェ・カラリス」は大量生産を頑なに拒んできたメーカーが1936年から生産する上質なアラビカコーヒー。イタリア19地方のパニーニも味わえるこのレストランでは、毎日食べたくなるようなイタリア料理も提供しています。

il caffè

"Please choose from our menu, or ask the waiter to serve almost anything from the shelves. Try it with Italian bread and something from today's deli counter."

MIA RIGO, PROPRIETOR

antipasti
all £8.50

BOARD OF MIXED ITALIAN MEAT

BOARD OF MIXED ITALIAN CHEESES

BOARD OF MIXED ITALIAN MARINATED VEGETABLES

or create your own combination

14 Gloucester Road
London SW7 4RB
020 7581 6964
www.miarigo.com

regional panini
all £4.50

choose from the 19 regions of Italy or we'll make your own combination

TRENTINO
speck, walnut paté, asiago cheese and olive oil

VALDOSTANO
bacon, fontina cheese, olive paté and marinated aubergine

FRIULANO
San Daniele ham, montasio cheese, red pesto and olive oil

PIEMONTESE
truffle oil, tuma cheese and Italian roast ham

LOMBARDO
bresaola, parmesan shavings, taleggio cheese and olive oil

VENETO
anchovy paté, tuna, rocket, mayonnaise, tomatoes and olive oil

LIGURE
pesto, pine nuts, mozzarella and roast ham

EMILIANO
culatello di zibello, stracchino cheese, walnuts, rocket and olive oil (this can also be made with piadina bread)

TOSCANO
bresaola, pecorino cheese, grilled vegetables, pepper and olive oil

LAZIALE
caprino cheese, truffle roast ham, marinated artichokes and olive oil

MARCHIGIANO
montasio cheese, coppa, green olive pate and olive oil

UMBRO
prosciutto di norcia, truffle pecorino cheese, butter and pepper

ABRUZZESE-MOLISANO
pecorino cheese, olive paté, pancetta and olive oil

BASILISCO
boar mortadella, pecorino cheese, caciocavallo cheese, olives and mushrooms

PUGLIESE
tuna, rocket, cherry tomatoes and buffalo mozzarella

CALABRESE
spicy salami, chilli, olive oil, scamorza cheese and sun dried tomatoes

CAMPANO
salame di Napoli, buffalo mozzarella, cherry tomatoes and oregano

SARDO
Sardinian pecorino cheese, salame and olive oil

SICILIANO
grilled aubergine, peppers, mozzarella, olives and olive oil

Menu メニュー

10% off

Please visit us soon and discover some of our entirely Italian food and wine. Just mention this leaflet and we'll give you a 10% discount on all food eaten here or taken away. (This offer does not include wines and drinks.) Find us at the Kensington Gardens end of Gloucester Road. We are open from 8am to 9pm from Monday to Saturday and 8am until 6pm on Sunday.

020 7581 6964
14 Gloucester Road, London SW7 4RB
www.miarigo.com

ENJOY!

This **free cantucci biscuit** is a tiny taste of what's in store at **Mia Rigo's**.

Please visit the top end of Gloucester Road for a stylish **salumeria, caffè** and **galleria**. Experience entirely **authentic Italian** produce, exclusive wines, and the best **Italian design**.

own **olive oil**

vinegar, or a

coffee with

Panini.

Canteen キャンティーン

Restaurant　レストラン
Unit 2 Crispin Place, Spitalfields,
▶ London E1 6DW
http://www.canteen.co.uk

Interior Design:Barber Osgerby　A:Universal Design Studio　Bespoke Furniture:Windmill Furniture (Brand name:Isokon)
Graphic Design, Web Design:Hudson Powell

Canteen is a restaurant that brings together the best in British food and British design in an informal all-day dinning environment.　Canteen is a democratic restaurant, the food is about simplicity and quality, the audience for Canteen is specific in neither age or gender but is made up of people with an appreciation of quality and value for money.

最高のイギリス料理とブリティッシュデザインを融合したキャンティーンは、いつでも食事が楽しめるカジュアル・スタイルのレストラン。シンプルで良質な料理を提供する庶民的なレストランです。世代や性別を問わず、値段に見合ったクオリティを求める人々に広く利用されています。

Leaflet
リーフレット

Menu　メニュー
Envelope　封筒

Postcard Teas ポストカード・ティーズ

Tea Importer and Retailer　紅茶輸入、販売

9 Dering Street, New Bond Street, London
▶ W1S 1AG
http://www.postcardteas.com

A, Interior Design:Bill Katz, Timothy d'Offay　CD, AD:Timothy d'Offay　LD:Timothy d'Offay, Anthony d'Offay, Peter B. Willberg　Graphic Design:Timothy d'Offay, Anthony d'Offay　P:Kenichi Nakao

Post Card
ポストカード

Leaflet
リーフレット

Postcard Teas is the result of 10 years travelling to 6 countries in Asia in search of the world's finest teas by Timothy d'Offay. It is a place where people can try these teas and find beautiful teaware much of which is made exclusively for us.

ポストカード・ティーズは、世界の極上のお茶を求めてアジア6ヵ国を10年かけて旅したティモシー・ドフェイの集大成と言えるお店。さまざまなお茶を試してみたり、美しいティーウェアを探したりできる場所です。このお店で扱っているティーウェアの多くは、特注品となっています。

Whittard of Chelsea

ウィタード・オブ・チェルシー

Marketing Director:Alison Miles   P:Kenichi Nakao

Tea and Coffee

紅茶、コーヒー

▶ 38 Covent Garden market, London WC2E 8RF
http://www.whaittard.co.uk

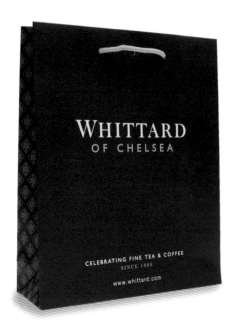

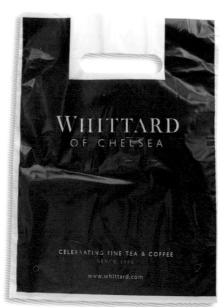

Whittard of Chelsea have been selling the finest tea and coffee from around the globe since 1886. To compliment this range Whittard also offer an extensive range of Tea and Coffee gift packs as well as ranges of ceramic ware which include a large variety of mugs, teapots and traditional cups and saucers. British tourist designs are also available in all ranges.

1886年以来、ウィタード・オブ・チェルシーは世界中から集めた極上の紅茶とコーヒーを販売してきました。また、紅茶やコーヒーのギフト用詰め合わせをはじめ、マグ、ティーポット、伝統的なカップ＆ソーサーといったさまざまな陶磁器類にいたるまで、幅広い商品を提供しています。土産物も各種取り揃えています。

ENGLISH
BREAKFAST
LEAF TEA

Strong Traditional

The Nation's favourite,
rich, strong and fresh.

Net Wt. 125 g ℮ 4.41 oz

ENGLISH ROSE
FLAVOURED
LEAF TEA

Flavoured Tea

Sweet rose flavoured
black tea.

Net Wt. 125 g ℮ 4.41 oz

Catalog
カタログ

The National Café ナショナル・カフェ
The National Dining Rooms ナショナル・ダイニングルーム

A, CD, Interior Design:David Collins

Cafe　カフェ /
Restaurant and Bakery　レストラン、ベーカリー

The National Gallery, Trafalgar
Square, London WC2N 4DN
http://www.nationalgallery.org.uk

<Cafe> A first class café de luxe, the National Café is a timeless yet glamorous interpretation of a traditional Viennese café and features a waiter-service brasserie, self-service dining hall, espresso bar and stunning private dining room.

<Restaurant> A decidedly British restaurant and bakery, The National Dining Rooms have a feel of understated elegance and have been designed to reflect the British heritage of the building and its regal location.

〈カフェ〉ナショナル・カフェは高級感あふれる贅沢なカフェ。時代を超えた存在でありながら、ウィーンの伝統的なカフェの雰囲気を素敵に演出しています。ウエイターが給仕をするブラッスリーをはじめ、セルフサービスのダイニング・ホール、エスプレッソ・バー、そして目を見張るような個室のダイニングも用意されています。

〈レストラン〉ナショナル・ダイニング・ルームはまさに正統派の英国調レストラン＆ベーカリー。落ち着いた気品を感じさせるこのレストランのデザインは、イギリスの文化遺産である建物と、ナショナルギャラリー内というロケーションの威厳を感じさせます。

Shop Card　ショップカード

Menu　メニュー

114

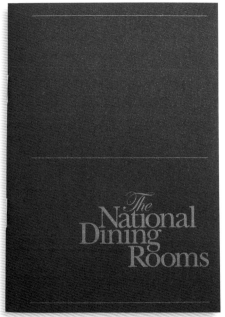

Leaflet　リーフレット

The National Dining Rooms

The National Dining Rooms is the restaurant and bakery situated in the Sainsbury Wing of London's National Gallery with views over Trafalgar Square. We are open from 10am – 5.30pm daily and for dinner on Wednesday evenings until 8.30pm.

The National Dining Rooms aims to provide the best in modern British cooking, using only fresh and seasonal ingredients sourced from producers from all over the British Isles. We are committed to supporting small-scale farmers, growers and cheese-makers wherever possible.

'County of the Month' in the Restaurant

There is a new eagerness to discover the provenance of our food coupled with a greater appreciation of the extraordinary diversity of British regional food. Virtually every corner of the British Isles yields superb produce with food varying greatly from region to region.

With this in mind, the restaurant at The National Dining Rooms has introduced 'County of the Month Menus'. These menus feature the very best regional ingredients sourced from rare breed farmers, specialist fisherman and cheesemakers from all over the British Isles. Produced to artisan methods in small quantities, this is a rare opportunity to sample the best of Great Britain.

July Menu – Kent
Salad of Heritage tomatoes with tarragon and pickled shallots.
Warm smoked salmon with courgettes and lemon.
Gilt-head bream baked with hops, served with new carrots and rainbow chard.
Organic Romney lamb with wet garlic and buttered potatoes.
Rice pudding with marinated Kent strawberries and basil.
Organic Basings goat's cheese with Kentish apple chutney and crispbreads.

August Menu – Yorkshire
Wild mushroom omelette with summer salad leaves.
York ham with Yorkshire relish and toasted rye bread.
Whitby cod with minted English peas and warm tartare sauce.
Roast wood pigeon with leeks and hazelnuts.
Yorkshire curd tart with drunken raisins.
Mature Wensleydale with fruit bread.

September Menu – Oxfordshire
Organic sweet corn soup infused with basil.
Coddled brown trout with Shaken Oak mustard and watercress.
Fillet of zander with Port Meadow crayfish sauce and glazed spring onions.
Oxford Sandy and Black pork with quince, cinnamon and bitter leaves.
Blackberry and apple crumble tartlet.
Oxford Blue with chutney and crispbreads.

The Bakery

Our bakery is open every day throughout the year for breakfast, elevenses, light lunches, drinks and quintessentially English afternoon teas.

We freshly bake every day so you can discover the great and often forgotten tradition of British baking. Indulge in great breads, old-fashioned cakes, sweet and savoury tarts and pies, as well as biscuits, sweet pots and pastries.

The Bakery offers a wide variety of regional British cheeses, from Sharpham Brie and Cornish Yarg to Lancashire Blackstick Blue to name but a few. We also serve a wide selection of drinks including English ales, New Forest ciders, fruit blends and smoothies as well as over 20 specially blended loose leaf teas.

Flyer　フライヤー

Paul A Young Fine Chocolates

ポール・エー・ヤング

Confectionery

お菓子

▶ 33 Camden Passage, Islington, London N1 8EA
http://www.payoung.net

Interior Design:Paul A Young   LD:Rik Gadsby, Sick Pixels   P:Akiko Watanabe

Sticker　ステッカー

Shop Card
ショップカード

We hand make contemporary and innovate chocolates including brownies, bars, hot chocolate and chocolate sculptures. We hold chocolate tastings with whisky, wine and tequilla, chocolate workshops and classes. We won best new UK chocolate shop in 2006, world chocolate awards along with two awards for our chocolates. All our produce are made by Paul on site in this purpose built chocolate kitchen.

ブラウニー、チョコバー、ホットチョコレート、チョコの彫刻など、現代的で斬新なチョコレートを作り、2つの賞を受賞しています。またウィスキー、ワイン、テキーラと味わう試食会やワークショップなども開催し、2006年UKベストチョコレートショップに選ばれました。全商品ポールが店の専用キッチンで作っています。

L'Artisan du Chocolat

ラルティザン・デュ・ショコラ ▶

Confectionery
お菓子
89 Lower Sloane Street, London SW1W 8DA
http://www.artisanduchocolat.com

CD, Interior Design:Anne-Francoise Weyns and Gerard Coleman   P:Akiko Watanabe

Our London store is located in the heart of Chelsea. Inside exotic rosewood and zebrano flirt with stainless steel, glass, slate and copper. We designed our shop with our sensibility: paying attention to details and choosing luxurious noble. Our chocolates like jewels are kept in refrigerated counters with sliding drawers that open towards you. The atmosphere we hope we have achieved is modern understated luxury, warmth and welcome.

チェルシーの中心にある店舗の内装はエキゾチックなシタン材とゼブラノ材にステンレス、ガラス、スレート、銅で遊び心をプラス。細部への配慮と贅沢な気品が感じられる繊細な設計。宝石のようなチョコはお客様側に引き出せる引き出し付き冷蔵ケースに。現代的で落ち着いた高級感と温かみのある雰囲気を創出しています。

Gaucho ガウチョ

Restaurant and Bar　レストラン, バー

Gaucho Picadilly, 19 Swallow Street,
London W1B 4DJ
http://www.gauchosgrill.com

A:Andrew Wilson　　CD:Patsy Godik　　AD:Darren Holburn　　D:Patsy Godik　　CW:Gioma Uk　　I:Darren Holburn − Patsy Godik
LD:Darren Holburn　P:Kenichi Nakao

Gaucho Piccadilly, recently awarded Best Steak Restaurant by Time Out Magazine 2006, is one of 7 very successful Argentine steak restaurants, owned by Zev Godik. Gaucho's interior designer, Patsy Godik has decorated the interiors with black glass chandeliers, black carpets, cow hide covered walls and chairs combine to create a stunning restaurant and bar on four floors.

2006年『Time Out』誌のベストステーキ店に選ばれたガウチョ・ピカデリーは、アルゼンチンステーキを出す人気7店舗のひとつ。オーナーはゼヴ・ゴディック。インテリアはパッツィ・ゴディックによるもので黒ガラスのシャンデリアや黒い絨毯、牛革張りの壁や椅子が相まって、4フロア構成のレストラン＆バーは見事な空間に。

CAVAS DE GAUCHO

25 Swallow Street, London W1B 4QR   T 020 7437 0895
F 020 7734 1876
E cavasdegaucho@gaucho-grill.com   www.gaucho-grill.com/cavasdegaucho

FOOD

Mo Tea Room モ・ティールーム

Tea Room and Retail
ティールーム、販売
5 Heddon Street, London W1B 4BH
http://www.momoresto.com

CD, AD, Interior Design:Mourad Mazouz   P:Kenichi Nakao

Post Card
ポストカード

Match
マッチ

Momo, named after the owner Mourad Mazouz, is a unique North African restaurant and has been highly successful for 10 years. Attracting diverse crowds, from London locals, tourists and A-List celebrities. The Mo Tearoom was set up in 1999 and attracts tea enthusiasts and shisha lovers. The whole site, has been decorated to resemble a beautiful souk, with wonderful lights, artifacts and pictures.

経営者ムラド・マズーズから名付けられたMomoは個性的な北アフリカ料理店。10年間、高い人気を保ち続け、地元民や旅行者、大物セレブたちをも魅了しています。99年にはMoをオープン。紅茶ファンや水タバコ（シーシャ）ファンを惹きつけています。照明、工芸品、絵が飾られた店内は、美しいスークを思わせます。

CD

Shish シシュ

Restaurant and Bar
レストラン、バー
▶ 71-75 Bishops Bridge Road, London W2 6BG
http://www.shish.com

Graphic Design:Flat Cap Marketing

Point Card
ポイントカード

Flyer　フライヤー

Using natural materials such as palm wood combined with contemporary furniture, the three Shish restaurants provide an ultra modern, relaxed and informal setting for one of the oldest cooking methods in the world. Light and airy spaces with floor to ceiling windows, the restaurants feature open plan kitchens, providing real theatre while diners watch the chefs at work, cooking on open flames.

ヤシなどの自然素材と現代的な家具を取り入れた非常にモダンな3つのレストランはカジュアルにくつろげる空間。歴史あるシルクロードの料理を提供します。天井から床まで開いた大窓により、軽快で開放的なスペースとなっています。特徴的なのはオープンキッチン。シェフが直火で料理するのを目の前で楽しむことができます。

Melt メルト

Confectionery
お菓子

▶ 59 Ledbury Road, London W11 2AA
http://www.meltchocolates.com

Interior Design:Louise Nason, Michaelis Boyd   A:Michaelis Boyd   CD, AD, D, LD, CW:Louise Nason
I:Ian Bilbey (Illustration for card)   P:Kenichi Nakao

A chocolate shop that will excite your senses! All the chocolates are made in the kitchen. They are fresh and made with excellent quality ingredients.

Meltはあらゆる感覚を刺激するチョコレートショップで、商品はすべて店内のキッチンで作っています。高品質の原料を使った新鮮なチョコレートを提供します。

Package　パッケージ

Shop Card
ショップカード

Le Pain Quotidien

ル・パン・コティディアン

Restaurant and Bakery　レストラン、ベーカリー

Marlborough Turner Building, 18 Great
Marlborough Street , London W1F 7HU
http://www.painquotidien.com

A, Interior Design:Stiff Trevillion　CD:Clare Sheppard　AD, LD:Alain Coumont　Graphic Design:Holger Jacobs
P:Kenich Nakao

Le Pain Quotidien is an organic bakery restaurant which provides inexpensive, quality food in a convivial rustic setting. We serve naturally-leavened, handmade bread made from organic flour. Our large communal table is the centre piece of our store. It is where people can sit, whether or with friends to converse and enjoy our food in the company of others.

素朴で明るい環境の中で、安くて質の高い食事を提供するオーガニック・ベイカリーレストラン。有機栽培の小麦を使って自然発酵させた焼き立てパンをお届けしています。店の真ん中には大きなテーブルがしつらえられていて、友達と語らいながら、食事を楽しめるスペースとなっています。

New Culture Revolution

ニュー・カルチャー・レボリューション

CD:David Lau　P:Kenich Nakao

Noodle and Dumpling Bar
ヌードル、飲茶
▶ 305 Kings Road, London SW3 5EP
http://www.newculturerevolution.co.uk

the dumpling & noodle bar

At the New Culture Revolution we put a strong emphasis on the proper combination of fresh ingredients, promoting good health, long life and energy through a delicate balance of starch, fibre, protein and vegetables. Our noodles are made fresh and exclusively for us. When we could not get good enough noodles in the UK, we sent someone back to Beijing to learn how they are made properly.

新鮮な材料を正確に組み合わせることに強いこだわりを持ち、でんぷん、繊維質、たんぱく質、野菜の絶妙なバランスにより健康、長寿、エネルギーを増進させます。麺は作りたての特製麺を使用。当初英国では入手できなかったため、スタッフが北京まで飛んで本格的な麺の製法を学んできた、というこだわりようです。

Menu　メニュー

Shop Card　ショップカード

Prêt-a-Portea at The Berkeley

プレタポルティー at バークレーホテル

Hotel, Tea Room
ホテル、ティールーム
▶ Wilton Place, Knightsbridge, London SW1X 7RL
http://www.the-berkeley.co.uk

A, Interior Design:Alexandra Champalimaud   P:Kenichi Nakao

Prêt-a-Portea is a new concept in afternoon tea served at The Berkeley. It has been designed to add a creative twist to the classic elements of the traditional English afternoon tea, with the cakes and pastries inspired by the latest fashion season's catwalk designs for the style conscious and with savouries in miniature mouthfuls for the figure conscious.

プレタ・ポルティーはバークレーで供されるアフタヌーン・ティーの新しいコンセンプト。英国の伝統であるアフタヌーン・ティーのクラシックな要素に独自のアレンジをプラス。お洒落に敏感な人には最新ファッションから着想を得たケーキやパティスリーを、体の線を気にする人には一口サイズ小さな軽食を用意しています。

Orange Pekoe Teas

オレンジ・ペコ・ティーズ ▶

Tea and Coffee
紅茶、コーヒー
3 White Hart Lane, Barnes, London SW13 OPX
http://www.orangepekoeteas.com

A, CD, AD, Interior Design, Graphic Design:Marianna Hadjigeorgiou & Achilleas Agridiotis
LD:Together Design Ltd   P:Yuki Sugiur

All our teas are single estate teas, directly from the tea gardens. Within our tea room we wanted to create an informal, relaxed atmosphere where people of any age or sex can come and feel comfortable to have a tea, lunch, cakes or traditional afternoon tea. We are strongly focused on selling all our 65 teas loose to customers and all our tea merchandise in our bespoke tea caddies and giftware.

全商品、単一の茶園で採れた新鮮な茶葉のみを使用。ティールームでは、老若男女問わず、お茶、ランチ、ケーキ、伝統的なアフタヌーン・ティーをゆったり楽しめる、カジュアルでリラックスした雰囲気を演出しています。65種のお茶はすべて量り売り可能で、オーダーメイドまたはギフト用パッケージで販売しています。

Tea Parlour at Sketch スケッチ・ティーパーラー ▶

Restaurant, Bar, Gallery & Tea Salon
レストラン、バー、ギャラリー、ティーサロン
9 Conduit Street, London W1S 2XG
http://www.sketch.uk.com

AD, Graphic Design:Mark Lawson Bell   CD:Mourad Mazouz   P:Yuki Sugiura

Menu
メニュー

Shop Card
ショップカード

Sketch is a complex and unique site, consisting of restaurants, bars, tea room and video art gallery. Conceived by French master chef Pierre Gagnaire and Algerian-born restauranteur Mazouz, it has attracted unprecedented media reaction for its myriad food, drink and surreal decorations since it opened in December 2002

レストラン、バー、ティールーム、ビデオアート・ギャラリーで構成されるユニークな複合施設。フレンチシェフ、ピエール・ガニエールとアルゼンチン生まれの経営者マズーズが築いたレストランは、2002年12月のオープン以来、種類豊富なフードやドリンクとシュールな内装でメディアから大きな注目を集めています。

Mash マッシュ

A, Interior Design:Andrew Martin

Restaurant and Bar
レストラン、バー
▶ 19-21 Great Portland Street, London W1W 8QA
http://www.mashbarandrestaurant.com

Leaflet　リーフレット

Letterhead　レターヘッド

Futuristic yet relaxed, Mash combines an opulent ground-floor bar complete with its very own micro- brewery, a funky first floor restaurant and offers everything from breakfast through to late-night cocktails.

フューチャリスティックでありながら、リラックスした雰囲気をかもし出すマッシュ。1階には、とても個性的な地ビールを出す華やかなバー、2階にはファンキーなレストランがあり、朝食から深夜のカクテルまで、さまざまな食事やドリンクを提供しています。

Les Trois Garcons レトワギャルソン

Restaurant
レストラン
1 Club Row, London E1 6JX
http://www.lestroisgarcons.com

A, CD, AD, Interior Design:Hassan Abdullah   LD:Brandinstinct   P:Kenichi Nakao

Post Card　ポストカード

A collaboration of ideas and interests between Antique dealers, designers, creative minds and restaurateurs who originally bought this old pub as a private house project. Filled with their sumptuous collection of treasures creates a decadent, romantic and at times, witty atmosphere. The restaurant opened its doors to the public in 2000 and has made an impression on everyone who walks through the door.

古いパブを個人邸に改装するプロジェクトとして始まり、骨董商、デザイナー、クリエイター、レストラン経営者のコラボレーションによって生まれたレストラン。店内にあふれる贅沢なコレクションは、退廃的でロマンティックで、ときにウィットに富んだ雰囲気を演出します。2000年に一般公開され、人々に感銘を与えています。

Leaflet　リーフレット

6 Little Portland Street
W1 W7JE London
Telephone: 020 7631 0700

LES TROIS ƷARÇOПS

1 Club Row
E1 6JX London
Telephone: 020 7613 1924

LOUNGELOVER

1 Whitby Street
E1 London
Telephone: 020 7012 1234

LES TROÌS ƷARÇOПS

St. John

セント・ジョーン

A, CD:In House P:Kenichi Nakao

Restaurant and Bakery
レストラン、ベーカリー
▶ 94-96 Commercial Street, London E1 6LZ
http://www.stjohnbreadandwine.com

Post Card　ポストカード

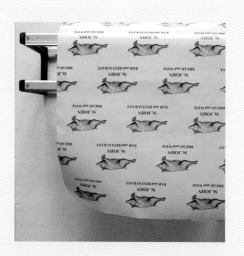

Bread and Wine came in a very calm natural way. Baking bread, serving wine, it seemed foolish not to sit down and enjoy both of the above, so it seemed amiss not to do some cooking to bond the two elements, thus it became a restaurant, much to our surprise. Hopefully the civilized pit stop we all need in life.

パンとワインが、ごく自然な形でさりげなく供されるレストラン。「パンを焼き、ワインを出すなら、その両方をゆっくり楽しまない手はない。それならパンとワインを結びつけるような料理を作るしかない」という発想からレストランという形態になったというのは意外。リフレッシュしたいときにうれしい小粋なレストランです。

Inn the Park イン・ザ・パーク

A, Interior Design:Hopkins Architects   CD:Tom Dixon

Cafe
カフェ

▶ St James's Park, London SW1A 1AA
http://www.innthepark.com

Sticking, contemporary and designed to blend harmoniously into the stunning landscape of St James' Park, Inn the Park offers a relaxed and friendly dining experience in one of London's most enchanting locations.

すばらしい風景が広がるセント・ジェームズ・パークに調和するようデザインされた、落ち着きのある現代的なレストラン、イン・ザ・パーク。ロンドン有数の魅力的なロケーションにあり、ゆったりくつろいだ雰囲気の中で食事を楽しむことができます。

Leaflet リーフレット

FASHION

Timothy Everest ティモシー・エヴェレスト

D:Timothy Everest P:Kenichi Nakao

Taylors
テーラー
▶ 35 Bruton Place, London W1
http://www.timothyeverest.co.uk

As one of the architects and leading practitioners of the new Bespoke Movement, Timothy Everest has spent the past decade introducing a new generation of men and women to the joys of handmade clothing. Located in a quiet street in the heart of Mayfair, the store provides Bespoke tailoring service and a small offering of ready made garments.

ニュービスポーク（新しいテーラーメイドのムーブメント）の旗手であり、その流れを実践するエヴェレストはこれまでの10年間、新しい世代の男女にハンドメイドの服のすばらしさを紹介してきました。メイフェアの閑静な通りに位置するショップでは、ビスポーク・テーラーのサービスに加え、少数の既製服も扱っています。

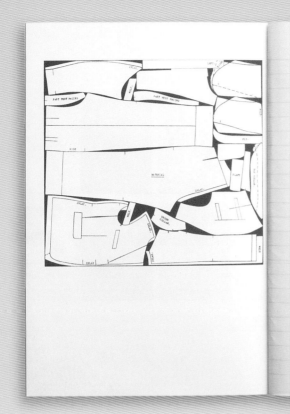

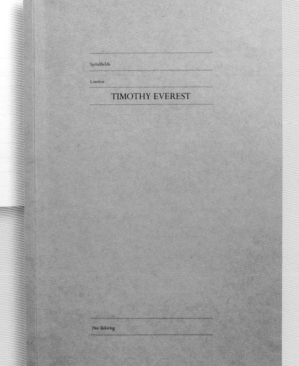

Catalog　カタログ

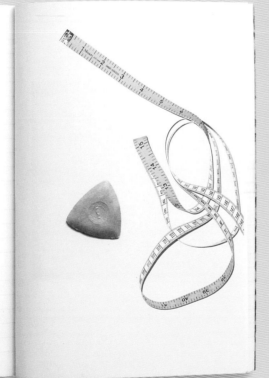

Hoxton Boutique

ホクストン・ブティック

CD:Alison Whalley P:Kenichi Nakao

Apparel
アパレル
▶ 2 Hoxton Street, London N1 6NG
http://www.hoxtonboutique.co.uk

HOXTON BOUTIQUE
2 HOXTON STREET
LONDON
N1 6NG
TEL 020 7684 2083 FAX 020 7684
E-MAIL; HOXTONBOUTIQUE@HOTMA

MON-FRI 10:30-6:30
11-6

TER 2006-2007
T, HUSSEIN CH
ROBERT CARY-W
, DR. DENIM
N AND MORE

Shop Card　ショップカード

Shopping Bag
ショッピングバッグ

Hoxton Boutique opened January 2000 in London's most exciting and creative area, Hoxton. A large gallery-like store, the interior is fabulously Studio 54 style, with mirrored walls, disco ball and neon lights. Always stocking the most exciting cutting edge designers, alongside established international labels.

ロンドンで最も刺激的でクリエイティブなエリアに、2000年1月にオープンしたホクストン。大きなギャラリーのようなショップは、鏡張りの壁、ミラーボールやネオンで飾られたゴージャスなディスコ「Studio 54」風のインテリア。最先端のデザイナーズアイテムや世界中の有名ブランドを扱っています。

Lola et Moi ローラ・エ・モア

CD, AD, D, CW:Rania Tohme　P:Kenichi Nakao

Children's Clothing
子供服

▶ 176 Walton Street, London SW3 2JL
http://www.lolaetmoi.com

Press Release
プレスリリース

Entering the world of "lola et moi" is getting back to the colorful, sparkling and candy-like world of childhood. Designed for girls from ages six months to twelve years, lola et moi creates vibrant separates inspired by retro patterns and traditional silhouettes and updated with fresh, unusual fabrics and whimsical adornments.

ローラ・エ・モアの世界感に触れると、カラフルでキラキラしたキャンディのような子ども時代に引き戻されます。ターゲットは生後6ヶ月から12歳までの女の子。レトロなパターンや伝統的なシルエットから発想し、これまでにない個性的なファブリックやユニークな装飾品で新しさを加えた、元気いっぱいの服を作っています。

Michel Guillon ミシェル・ギュイヨン

Eye Boutique and Vision Clinic 眼鏡、眼科
35 Duke of York Square, Sloane Square
London SW3 4LY
▶ http://www.michelguillon.com

LD, Interior Design:Ab Rogers of ARD   Director:Dr Michel Guillon   P:Kenichi Nakao

Michel Guillon, a pioneering eye-research scientist with over twenty-five years of experience, has developed a unique eye examination routine, which brings the forefront of technology to the high-street. The new Michel Guillon Vision Clinic in Sloane Square, features the latest eye testing technology and state-of-the-art equipment to create an eye-care service which is not readily available in the high street.

眼研究のパイオニアで25年のキャリアをもつ科学者ミシェル・ギュイヨンが独自の眼検査法を開発したことで、中心街に先端技術がもたらされました。スローン・スクエアにある新しいミシェル・ギュイヨン・ヴィジョン・クリニックの特徴は、最新視力検査技術と市街地ではなかなか受けられない最先端の眼科治療です。

Leaflet
リーフレット

Post Card　ポストカード

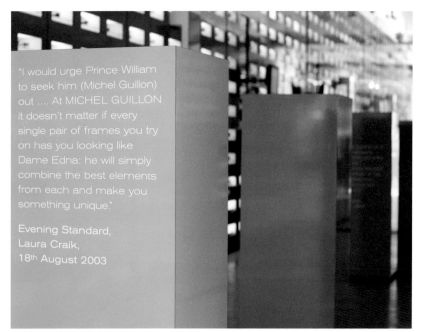

"I would urge Prince William to seek him (Michel Guillon) out .... At MICHEL GUILLON it doesn't matter if every single pair of frames you try on has you looking like Dame Edna: he will simply combine the best elements from each and make you something unique."

Evening Standard,
Laura Craik,
18th August 2003

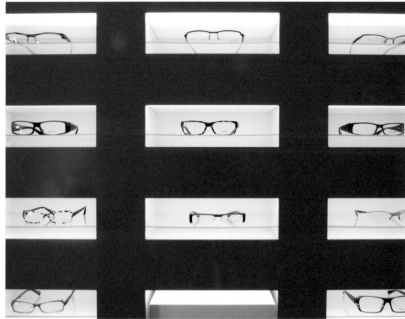

MICHEL GUILLON

Ally Capellino アリー・カペリーノ

CD, AD, LD:Alison Lloyd P:Akiko Watanabe

Apparel
アパレル
▶ 9 Calvert Avenue, London E2 7JP
http://www.allycapellino.co.uk

Ally Capellino is based in the heart of Shorditch . Ally produces two seasonal Mens and Womens collections a year . Our understated designs range from traditional wax cotton Satchels, smooth leather travel and work bags. Ally Capellino has a worldwide reputation for classic design & craftmanship.

ショーディッチの中心に拠点を置くアリー・カペリーノは、年2回、メンズ＆レディース・コレクションを制作。伝統的なワックスコットンのショルダーから、滑らかな革の旅行用＆ビジネス用まで、落ち着いたデザインのバッグを展開しています。クラシックなスタイルと職人技により世界的な名声を得ているブランドです。

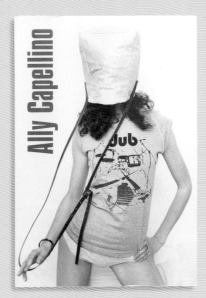

Ally Capellino

Men's Accessory Collection Spring/Summe

London Fashion Week 18-22 September 2005
Natural History Museum, Cromwell Road
London SW7
www.londonfashionweek.co.uk

Tranoi 6-9 October 2005
Bourse de Commerce, 2 Rue de Viarmes
75001 Paris
info@tranoi.com

London Showroom from 18th July 2005
5 Calvert Ave, London E2 7JP
t. +44 (0) 20 7613 3073
f. +44 (0) 20 7613 4519
e. info@allycapellino.co.uk
w. www.allycapellino.co.uk

Milan Showroom from 18th July 2005
Goa Corporation, Via A Sciesa 22
20135 Milano

th Sept 2005
ssaae

Photographe

Post Card　ポストカード

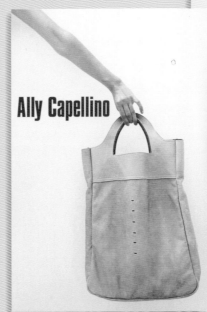

Post Card　ポストカード

Catalog　カタログ

Mootich ムーティック

Shoemaking and Retail
靴作り、靴
▶ 34 Elizabeth Street, London SW1
http://www.mootich.com

A, Interior Design:Mootich & friends　CD:Katarina Mootich　AD:Anna Sudbina　LD:Mootich　Graphic Design:Bogi
P:Akiko Watanabe

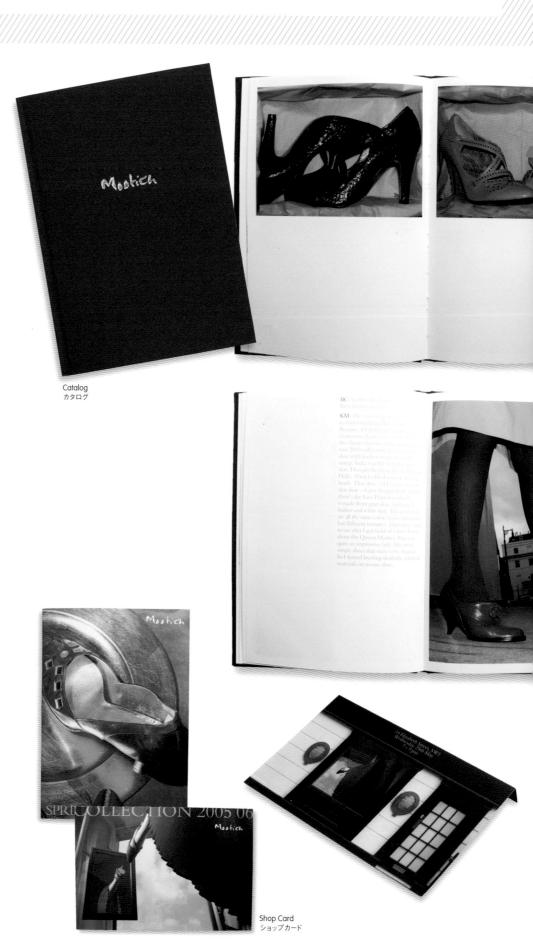

Catalog
カタログ

Mootich is a workshop for making shoes and a store carrying Katarina Mutich's ready wear shoe collections. In additon, it serves as an independent inspirational space in order to give base to individual talents in more productive manner - supporting the most talented and genuine artists to give them conditions to work in their best capacity.

靴作りのワークショップとカタリナ・ムーティックの既製靴を扱うショップを併設したムーティック。個人作家に、より生産的な方法で制作拠点を与えることを目指し、創造力をかきたてるようなスペースを提供しています。才能をいかんなく発揮できるような環境を与えることで、優秀なアーティストたちをサポートしています。

Shop Card
ショップカード

b Store ビー・ストア

Apparel
アパレル

▶ 24 A, Saville Row, London W1
http://www.bstorelondon.com

Lighting:Commitee Furniture:Peter Jensen, Siv Stoldal, Madelaine King CD, AD:Matthew Murphy, Kirk Beattie
P:Kenichi Nakao

Press Release
プレスリリース

b store has been a mecca for new fashion talent since opening in 2000,and it just got brighter with the new Savile Row boutique. Furniture and fittings have been designed by long-standing selling at b Store, including Bernhard Willhelm, Peter Jensen and Siv Stoldal. A Special 'shoe wall' was made by furniture designer Madelaine King for their house shoe brand, b Footwear.

2000年の開店以来、新鋭デザイナーが集まるファッションの中心的存在で、サヴィル・ローに移転しさらに充実しました。家具類は、B.ウィルヘルム、P.イェンセン、S.ストルダルら人気デザイナーによるもので、「靴の壁」は家具作家マドレーヌ・キングが、自社ブランド「bフットウェア」のために制作したものです。

Kirk Originals

カーク・オリジナルズ

Optical Boutique　眼鏡

29 Floral Street, Covent Garden, London
WC2E 9DP
▶ http://www.kirkoriginals.com

A, Interior Design:Jason and Karen Kirk　　CD:Jason Kirk　　AD, LD, Graphic Design:Karen Kirk　P:Kenichi Nakao

Shop Card　ショップカード

Our concept is that eyewear should be enjoyed, a pleasurable item of clothing rather than a medical device. Our designs are unique, bold, colourful and a confident statement of independence. Environment is as important as the product itself and we aim to reflect that in our store design.

メガネは、視力を補う器具というよりも、お洒落として楽しむためのものである、というのがカーク・オリジナルズのコンセプト。ユニークかつ大胆で、華やかなデザインは、独立心を堂々と表現しています。また、商品と同じぐらい大切なのが店の雰囲気であると考え、店内のインテリアにもこのコンセプトを反映しています。

KIRK ORIGINALS
eyewear designers

Histoire-de-Voir
Visor £170
Sun Lenses £245

Mackintosh and Globe-Trotter

マッキントッシュ・グローブトロッター

A, Interior Design:Taisuke Higuchi   P:Akiko Watanabe

Dual Concept Store
デュアルコンセプトストア
54-55 Burlington Arcade, Mayfair,
London W1J 0LB
http://www.globe-trotterltd.com

Located in the historic arcade in Piccadilly, "Mackintosh and Globe Trotter" is a dual concept store of two modern-day classic English brands. Mackintosh is known for developing the process of spreading rubber onto cotton to create the world's first formal waterproof fabric. Globe Trotter also hand made luxury luggage entirely constructed from vulcan fibre, a hand made ash wood frame, cloth lining and leather trimming.

ピカデリーの歴史あるアーケードにある、2つのコンセプトを持つ店。綿にラバーを塗布し世界初の防水生地を開発したマッキントッシュと、バルカンファイバー、手製アッシュウッドフレーム、布の内張り、革製トリミングを施した高級ハンドメイド旅行鞄で有名なグローブトロッターという英国を代表する2ブランドの専門店。

Shop Card
ショップカード

GLOBE-TROTTER

Rhapsody in Blue

In the beginning there was Brown. Whereas other suit case manufacturers were producing these standard colour cases, Globe-Trotter took it upon itself to stand out in the crowd. Although the definitive construction and styling of the Globe-Trotter suit cases remains the same today, in the early 1900s travel was widely associated with sea and air, the colour blue. So it was that Globe-Trotter suit cases of this bygone era became available in revolutionary Navy. This bold move in changing colour would go on to become a Globe-Trotter trademark.

Sail Away
CRUISE

Reminiscent of launching ship and setting sail on the high seas, the Cruise line is a fresh royal blue with contrasting navy blue leather belts and corner details. Inspired by yacht races in the Isle of Wight, just open the case and the lining with royal blue pin stripes on snow-white cotton cloth instantly reflects cool summer living.

GLOBE-TROTTER
HAND MADE LUXURY LUGGAGE
MADE IN ENGLAND · SINCE 1897

Black

Green & Tan

Navy Blue

Orange & Tan

Loop ループ

CD, D:Susan Cropper　　LD, Graphic Design (Website) :Goldtop　　P:Akiko Watanabe

Knitting
編み物
▶ 41 Cross Street, Islington, London N1 2BB
http://www.loop.gb.com/

Point Card
ポイントカード

Sticker
ステッカー

Shop Card
ショップカード

I opened Loop with the dream that it would be a knitter's haven and heaven. We have all kinds of knitting classes and stock beautiful designer products from independent designers working in knit and crochet. We have quirky homeware, children's things, toys and objects. It's a very cosy space with a log fire and baskets brimming with yarn and fairy lights in the window.

編み物好きのパラダイスにしたいという想いでオープンしたショップ。さまざまな編み物教室を開催している他、個人作家による美しいニットやカギ針編みの作品をはじめ、個性的な部屋着、子供向け雑貨、おもちゃなども扱っています。暖炉があり、毛糸がたくさん入ったバスケットが置かれ、電飾が窓辺を飾る心地よい空間です。

Tracey Neuls トレーシー・ニュールズ

Footwear
靴

▶ 29 Marylebone Lane, London W1U 2NQ
http://www.tn29.com

CD, AD, D, Interior Design:Tracey Neuls   LD, CW:Crawford Bryce   P:Kenichi Nakao

Shoe Box
シューボックス

Novelty
ノベルティ

Catalog
カタログ

Tracey Neuls is a retail space which ignores convention. With an unorthodox display of hanged shoes from the ceiling, it encourages people to touch and explore them. The 360 degrees view challenges perspective. "My shoes are whole objects, not half stories and that's how they should be experienced" - Tracey Neuls.

天井から靴をぶらさげるという型破りなディスプレイにより、靴を手に取ったり、じっくり眺めたりしやすくなっています。商品をあらゆる角度から見る、それは視点への挑戦です。「私の作る靴は、完結した、ひとつの完全なるもの。だから、その全体を体験してほしい」とトレイシー・ニュールズは語ります。

Couverture クーベルチュール

Clothing and Lifestyle
洋服、生活雑貨
▶ 310 King's Road, Chelsea, London SW3 5UH
http://www.couverture.co.uk

CD,AD:Emily Dyson   LD:Cherry Goddard   Graphic Design:In house   P:Kenichi Nakao

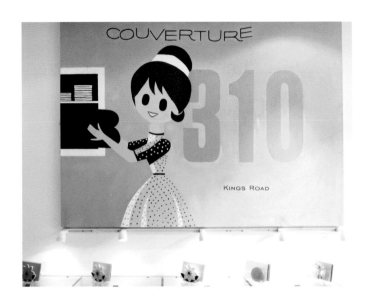

Shop Card
ショップカード

Flyer フライヤー

Established in 1999, Couverture specialises in covetable one-off designer pieces for the home, European fashion collections for women, cute knitted toys and children's clothing and accessories, as well as an ever changing flow of vintage finds.

1999年に創立したクーベルチュールでは、人気の高い一点もののデザイン雑貨（インテリア雑貨）から、ヨーロッパのレディースアパレル、毛糸でつくったおもちゃ、子ども服やアクセサリーまでを扱う専門店で、さまざまなビンテージの掘り出し物も次々に入荷しています。

Best ベスト

CD:Nicky Waddon P:Brent Darby

Design, Clothing and Art
デザイン、洋服、アート

▶ No5 Back Hill, London EC1R 5EN
http://www.bestshopever.com

Flyer フライヤー

Founded by Nicky Waddon, Best shop is about the Best of everything...design, illustration, Graffiti, books, magazines, clothing, accessories, Toys, prints...Every six weeks we turn the store into an exhibition space for already established and emerging artists.

ニッキー・ワドゥンが創業したベストショップは、デザイン、イラスト、グラフィティ、本や雑誌から、洋服、アクセサリー、おもちゃ、プリントまで、あらゆる分野のベスト商品を取り揃えるショップ。6週間ごとに、有名なアーティストや新進気鋭の若手作家などのエキシビションを開催しています。

DPMHI ディー・ピー・エム・エイチ・アイ

Clothing, Book, Art and Toys
洋服、本、アート、おもちゃ
▶ 2-3, Great Pulteney Street, Soho, London W1F 9LY
http://www.dpmhi.com

A, Interior Design:Francois Scali   CD:Hardy Blechman   P:Kenichi Nakao

Dpmhi is the flagship store for the mhi label as well as being dedicated to camouflage. It also houses a book department that stocks specialist titles on art and design, and a toy department with the largest range of contemporary designer toys. The dpmhi gallery in the store stages regular exhibitions which have included Jay One, graffiti legend Futura and skateboard star Mark Gonzales.

DPMHIはMHIレーベルの主要店舗で、迷彩柄に特化したショップ。芸術書やデザイン書を集めた本部門、現代的なデザイナートイの品揃えが豊富なおもちゃ部門もあります。店内のギャラリーでは、ジェイ・ワン、伝説的グラフィティ作家フューチュラ、スケボー界のヒーロー、マーク・ゴンザレスらの展覧会も定期的に開催。

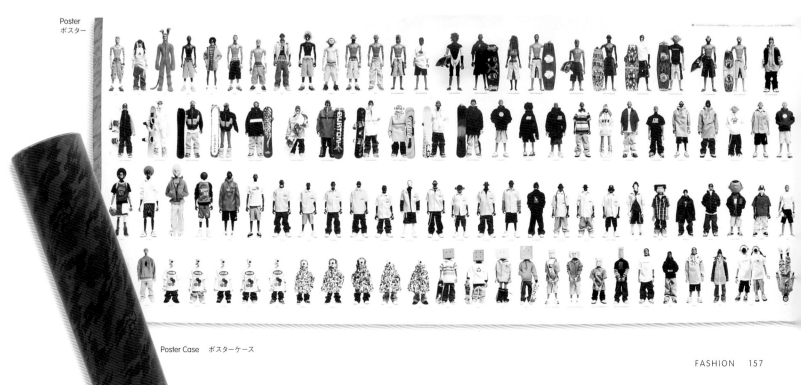

Poster
ポスター

Poster Case　ポスターケース

Reiss ライス

AD, LD, Graphic Design:Made Thought   A:d-raw

Apparel
アパレル
▶ 30-32 Islington Green, London N1 8DU
http://www.reiss.co.uk

Shop Card　ショップカード

Catalog　カタログ

Reiss is an UK-based fashion brand that positions itself between the high street multiples and the designer luxury brands. Retailing both menswear and womenswear, the collections are very directional, complemented by unique store locations and creative store environments. MadeThought are the appointed brand directors for Reiss, and are responsible for all aspects of visual branding, ranging from in-store graphical infection, campaign art-direction, packaging.

チェーン店と高級ブランドとの間を狙った英国ベースのファッションブランド。ユニークな立地、独創的な雰囲気と相まって、個性的なコレクションを展開。ブランドディレクターはMadeThought。店内グラフィック、キャンペーンアート、パッケージ、印刷物、広告など、すべてのヴィジュアル・ブランディングを手がけています。

Catalog　カタログ

Catalog　カタログ

Start London スタート・ロンドン

Apparel
アパレル

▶ 42-44 Rivington Street, London EC2A 3BN
http://www.start-london.com

Interior Design:Phillip Oakley　　CD, AD:Phillip Start and Brix Smith Start　　Graphic Design:Emak Mafu　　P:Kenichi Nakao

Shop Card　ショップカード

Philip's background in retail (founder of Woodhouse) and Brix's rock 'n' roll pedigree (former singer, song writer and guitarist for cult band The Fall), combine to give Start it's unique personality – Start is where 'Fashion meets Rock 'n' Roll'. Customers are treated as friends and come for the personal service and exceptional variation of new and interesting products whether it be jewellery, skincare, quirkier luxury brands or new clothing labels.

小売業者フィリップ（ウッドハウス創設者）とロッカーのブリックス（カルトバンド「ザ・フォール」の元メンバー）の経験が合体し、独特の個性が誕生しました。ファッションとロックの融合です。フレンドリーで細やかな対応と、ジュエリーからスキンケア、奇抜な高級ブランドや新しいブランドまで、豊富な品揃えが魅力です。

Mirage, Knightsbridge

ミラージュ・ナイツブリッジ

Apparel (Ladies)

アパレル（レディース）

▶ 193-195 Brompton Road, London SW3 1LZ
http://www.miragelondon.com

Interior Design:Doron Zilkha CD:Valeria Zilkha LD,Graphic Design:Rashna Mody-Clark P:Kenichi Nakao

Mirage was born out of a vision by Valeria Zilkha who with over 20 years experience in fashion envisioned a non segmented multi brand store. With Mirages's own brand of knitwear combined with some of the most exclusive names in fashion Barbara Bui, Atsuro Tayama, Gaetanno Navarra just to name a few Mirage offers a luxurious collection season after season.

ファッション界で20年以上の経験をもつヴァレリア・ジルカのヴィジョンから生まれたセレクトショップ。ニットウェアのオリジナルブランドとともに、バルバラ・ビュイ、アツロウタヤマ、ガエタノ・ナヴァラなど代表的な高級ブランドを取り揃え、毎シーズン、ゴージャスなコレクションを提供しています。

Matthew Williamson

マシュー・ウィリアムソン

CD, Interior Design:Matthew Williamson   P:Akiko Watanabe

Apparel (Ladies)
アパレル（レディース）
▶ 28 Bruton Street, London W1J 6QH
http://www.matthewwilliamson.co.uk

MATTHEW WILLIAMSON

28 Bruton Street
London
W1J 6QH
Tel: 020 7629 6200
Fax: 020 7629 6202
www.matthewwilliamson.com

Our store gives the whole Matthew Williamson experience. It is a fusion of the old and new, synthetic and natural. The effect is exotic, unexpected and a little magical with dazzling embellishment and modern clean lines. We recently opened a section within the store which is a bijou limited collection made up of vintage pieces I have found.

マシュー・ウィリアムソンを堪能できるショップ。古と新、人工物と自然とが融合しています。エキゾチックで意外性があって、うっとりするような装飾とシンプルでモダンなラインがほどこされた店内は、どこか幻想的。このほど、ヴィンテージの宝石を用いたアクセサリーの限定コレクションのコーナーが設置されました。

Look Book
ルックブック

Solange Azagury-Partridge

ソランジュ・アザグリー・パートリッジ

Jewellery
ジュエリー

▶ 187 Westbourne Grove, London W11 2SB

A, Interior Design:Solange Azagury-Partridge and Wells Mackereth Architects   CD, AD:Solange Azagury-Partridge
LD:Alan Aldridge   Graphic Design:Michael Nash Associates

Novelty
ノベルティ

"One day every woman wakes up wanting diamonds," believes jewelry designer, Solange Azagury-Partridge whose aesthetic approach has been described as iconoclastic, irreverent and phenomenal. Solange opened her shop in Westbourne Grove in 1995. The store designed as an oversized jewellery box, immediately attracted an international, eclectic client base spanning the likes of endless rock gods and goddesses to artists, filmmakers and anyone with an unconventional approach to beauty.

S.アザグリ・パートリッジの美しさへのアプローチは、型破り、不敬、驚異的などと形容されます。1995年にウエストボーン・グローブにオープンしたショップは巨大な宝石箱のようで、瞬く間にロック界のスターやアーティスト、映画監督など、美に対して個性的なアプローチをしている世界中の人々を惹きつけました。

Maharishi, Covent Garden, London

マハリシ・コベントガーデン・ロンドン

Apparel　アパレル
19 Floral Street, Covent Garden, London
WC2E 9HL
http://www.emaharishi.com

A, Interior Design:Francois Scali　CD:Hardy Blechman　P:Kenichi Nakao

Business Card
名刺

dpmhi
2-3 GPS
Great Pulteney Street
Soho, London W1F 9LY
tel +44 (0) 207 494 7550
fax +44 (0) 871 218 0262
www.dpmhi.com
gpstore@dpmhi.com

Shop Card　ショップカード

The maharishi store holds the men's, women's and denim collections. Covering two floors, the product sits alongside visual artwork from current and past collaborators, including camouflage beanbags and graffiti based paintings. Books displayed above the rails reflect Maharishi's ethos. The Churchill gallery creates an opportunity for guest artists contributing to the clothing collections to showcase their work, as well as other artists who best reflect Maharishi's interests and beliefs. Previous exhibitors have included Futura and Henry Chalfant.

メンズ／レディースのデニムを扱うマハリシは2フロア構成。商品とともに、迷彩柄ビーズクッションやグラフィティなどコラボレーターの作品や、ブランド理念を表す本をディスプレイ。チャーチルギャラリーはデザイン協力した作家やブランドイメージに合う作家の発表の場で、フューチュラやH.チャルファントの展覧会も開催。

Mallon & Taub マロン&ターブ

Optical Boutique　眼鏡、コンタクトレンズ

35D Marylebone High Street, Marylebone,
London W1U 4QB
▶ http://mallonandtaub.com

Interior Design:Huw Davies　CD, AD, LD, Graphic Design:Joan Mallon / Shanah Taub　P:Yuki Sugiura

We wanted a warm, comfortable environment where one could
freely view and try designer eyewear and sunglasses and feel
instantly relaxed. Pale, delicate olive panels create a contrast
against the bright backdrop of the main structural walls. The
colour scheme is combined with an Italian Grey slate floor and
black American walnut cabinets.

デザイナーズアイウェアやサングラスを自由に見て、試せて、店に入
ったとたん安らげるような、温かくて心地よい店づくりを目指しました。
繊細な青のオリーブパネルが明るい壁とコントラストをなしています。
イタリア製のグレーのスレート床と米国製のブラックウォルナット材
のキャビネットに合わせた配色を採用しています。

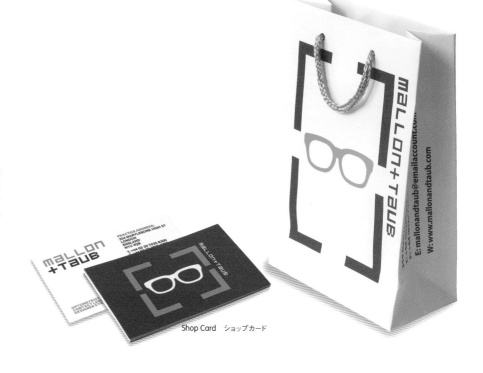

Shop Card　ショップカード

SERVICE

The Zetter ゼッター

Hotel　ホテル

▶ St Johns Square, 86-88 Clerkenwell Road,
London EC1M 5RJ
http://www.thezetter.com

AF, Interior Design:Precious McBane　Graphic Design:Fabian Monheim　P:Brent Darby

The Zetter is located in a converted 19th century Clerkenwell warehouse consisting of 59 bedrooms, a modern Mediterranean restaurant & 2 private rooms. The Zetter is sandwiched between the East and West End – a destination with style, comfort and personality without the price tag.

ゼッターは、19世紀に建てられたクラークンウェルの卸売問屋を改装したホテル。59のベッドルーム、モダンな地中海レストラン、2つのプライベート・ルームを備えています。イーストエンドとウエストエンドの間に位置するこのホテルは、センスよく、快適で、特別な価値のある空間を提供しています。

Bar Tapas Menu

Cheese & charcuterie
Octopus, celery & potato salad
Olive & salami croquette
Rocket & parmesan salad
Home cured salmon & pumpkin blinis
Grilled provolone & panzanella
Marinated olives/ Fried corn kernels / Fried
with chilli

Beers

Moretti - Italy 4.6%
Heineken - Holland 5.0%
Meantime Pale Ale - England 4.7%
Meantime Union Amber Lager - England
Meantime Wheat Beer - England 6.3%

Aperitifs

Martini Bianco / Extra Dry / Rosso
Noilly Prat
Campari
Pernod
Pimms
Aperol

Sherries

Deliciosa Manzanilla Sherry
Inocente Fino Sherry
Tio Diego Dry Amontillado Sherry
Don Gonzalo Oloroso Sherry

An optional service charge of 12.5% will be added to the bill.

Menu メニュー

Leaflet
リーフレット

Spots Dry Cleaners

スポッツ・ドライ・クリーナーズ ▶

Dry Cleaning
クリーニング
264 Upper Street, Islington, London N1 2UQ
http://www.spotsdrycleaners.com

LD, CW, Interior   Design:In House   P:Akiko Watanabe

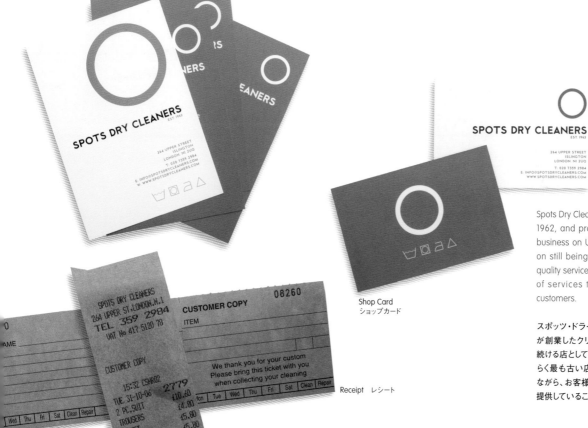

Shop Card
ショップカード

Receipt   レシート

Spots Dry Cleaners was founded by Mr. M Eshref back in 1962, and probably remains the oldest family owned business on Upper Street, Islington. We pride ourselves on still being a family business that provides a high quality service to all of our customers, and a wide range of services that meets all cleaning needs of our customers.

スポッツ・ドライ・クリーナーズは、1962年にM.エシュレフ氏が創業したクリーニング店。いまだ昔ながらの家族経営を続ける店としては、イズリントンのアッパー・ストリートでおそらく最も古い店でしょう。家族で切り盛りしている店でありながら、お客様の要望に応える幅広いサービスを高品質で提供していることに誇りをもっています。

Lund Olser ランド・オスラー

A, Interior Design:Powell Tuck Associates (Lund Osler Dental Health) CD:Julian Powell Tuck & Angus Shepherd (Lund Osler Dental Health)
A, Interior Design:B3 Designers Ltd (Smile and Skin, Face by Lund Osler) CD:Mark Bithrey (Smile and Skin, Face by Lund Osler) P:Kenichi Nakao

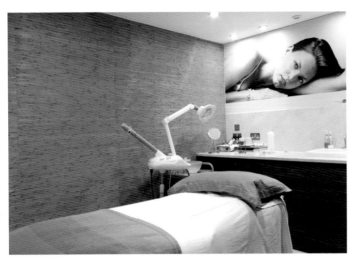

Shop Card　ショップカード

Letterhead　レターヘッド

172

Specialised Facial Aesthetic Surgeon available for comprehensive consultations and direct appointments.

DERMAL
AESTHETICS

· Consultation
· Lip Sculpting
· Line and Wrinkle
  Reduction Treatments
· Botox
· Anti Wrinkle
· Non surgical treatments
· Tissue re supporting
· Lifting treatments
· Facial cosmetic procedures

Dr Jerry Farrier is a qualified maxofacial surgeon and plastic surgeon. He has a wealth of experience and has completed the Aesthetic Surgery Fellowship in Cambridge.

Smile by Lund Osler

Leaflet　リーフレット

Letterhead
レターヘッド

Perfect your smile…

Catalog　カタログ

To create an environment that is seamless and minimalist, breaking the traditional concepts of health related environments to allow our clients to feel welcome, positive and experience a journey to be remembered as well as experiencing quality care and service. Thus creating a positive mind set and helping with their inner psyche which would in turn have a positive impact on their treatment and healing and an overall balance of mind and matter.

健康に関する従来の概念を捨て、スムーズでミニマルな環境をつくることで、お客様に温かく明るい雰囲気を感じてもらい、心に残る体験、質の高いケアやサービスを受けてもらうことができます。このことがポジティブ思考を生み、心理的サポートにつながるため、治療効果が高まり、心と体のバランスにプラスの影響を与えます。

Myhotel マイホテル

Hotel ホテル

11-13 Bayley Street, Bedford Square,
London WC1B 3HD
► http://www.myhotels.com

A, Interior Design:Conran & Partners   CD:James Soane   AD:Future City   LD:Imagination   Graphic Design:Zahrol Sanif
P:Kenichi Nakao

Shop Card
ショップカード

myhotels are lifestyle hotels which recognise that people are the
balancing point of pivotal design. Using the principles of feng shui
guests experience the harmony of sound, light, colour, aroma,
texture and taste. "Heaven they say is in the detail and that's
something the people at myhotels never forget" Andy
Thrasyvoulou, founder of myhotels.

変化を伴う設計においてバランスポイントとなるのは人である、とい
う考えの下に展開するライフスタイル・ホテル。風水を取り入れたこ
のホテルのゲストは音、光、色、香、触感、味のハーモニーを体験しま
す。創業者アンディ・スラシヴルは言います。「極楽は細部に宿る──
このことを当ホテルスタッフは肝に銘じています」

Letterhead   レターヘッド
Post Card   ポストカード

Catalog
カタログ

my energy

www.myhotels.com

Letterhead
レターヘッド

i like
it clean

(please service my room)

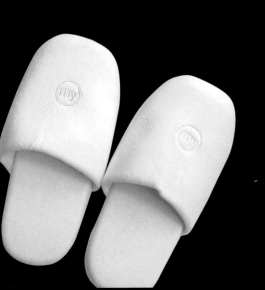

Catalog
カタログ

bedrooms & suites
78 stylish rooms - all with air-conditioning, flat screen TVs, CD players and welcoming music, tea and coffee making facilities, bottled water, hair dryer, Aveda blends, a complimentary daily newspaper and magazines.

myplace
a unique two-bedroom urban penthouse suite with its own kitchen and a fantastic roof terrace. One of London's coolest bedrooms.

mybar Bloomsbury
a lively informal bar serving breakfast, lunch, dinner and memorable cocktails. Open 24/7 to hotel guests.

myhotel Bloomsbury
11-13 Bayley Street
Bedford Square
London WC1B 3HD
t +44 (0)20 7667 6000
f +44 (0)20 7667 6001
e bloomsbury@myhotel

myhotel Chelsea
35 Ixworth Place
London SW3 3QX
t +44 (0)20 7225 7500
f +44 (0)20 7225 7555
e chelsea@myhotels.co

For all your reservation
please contact

myhotels Central Res
myhq
36 Bedford Square
London WC1B 3EL
t +44 (0)20 7637 2000
f +44 (0)20 7667 6000
e res@myhotels.com

myhotels.com

Calmia

Holistic Lifestyle Store and Tea Bar

カルミア

Spa, Cosmetic Store and Tea Bar

スパ、化粧品、ティーバー

▶ 52-54 Marylebone High Street, London W1U 5HR
http://www.calmia.com

A, Interior Design:Groves Natches   AD, LD:In house

Our vision is to relieve your stress and relax you by creating moments of everyday tranquillity. We achieve this by providing a range of spa services and related products, enabling you to seamlessly and effortlessly fit the spa lifestyle experience into your everyday life.

日常の中に静かで安らかな時間をつくり出すことにより、人々をストレスから解放し、リラックスしてもらいたい──そんなビジョンを達成すべく、スパをはじめ、癒しに関連するさまざまな商品を提供。毎日の生活の中に、無理なく手軽にスパ体験を取り入れられるようなサービスを展開しています。

Taylor Taylor London

テイラー・テイラー・
ロンドン

▶

Hair, Beauty and Grooming Salon
美容室
137 Commercial Street, London E1 6BJ
http://www.taylortaylorlondon.com

A, CD, AD, Interior Design:Bradley Taylor LD, P:Steve Langley

Price list
値段表

Leaflet　リーフレット

The Taylor Taylor Style Sanctuary is the ultimate urban retreat where clients can expect to be pampered in luxurious surroundings in the hands of some of the industry's most sought after stylists and beauticians. Highlights include a floor to ceiling gold tiled washroom as well as a stunning open cocktail bar and lounge.

テイラーテイラー・スタイル・サンクチュアリは、まさに都会にたたずむ究極のオアシス。贅沢な空間の中、業界きっての売れっ子スタイリストや美容師によるサービスを堪能できます。床から天井までゴールドのタイルで仕上げられた洗面所と目の覚めるようなオープンカクテルバー＆ラウンジがこのサロンの最大の特徴です。

Tendental テンデンタル

Dental Practice
歯医者

▶ 10 The Pavement, Clapham Common, London SW4 OHY
http://www.tendental.com

Interior Design:Andy Smith   LD:Tamsin Loxley   CD:DR Martin Wanendeya & DR Nikhil Sisodia   P:Brent Darby

Member's Card
メンバーズカード

Leaflet
リーフレット

what we do, who we are and how we work

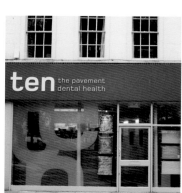

Tendental is a partnership of two dentists Dr Nikhil Sisodia and Dr Martin Wanendeya. Their aim was to provide Clapham with a modern stylish dental practice that offers exceptionally high standards of dental care with the provision of on site specialist services.

テンデンタルは、Dr.ニキル・シソーディアとDr.マーティン・ワネンデヤという2人の歯科医師が共同で開設した歯科医院です。ロンドンのクラパム地区に、極めて高いレベルの歯科治療と専門家によるサービスを提供する、スタイリッシュで近代的な歯科医院を開くことを目的として開設されました。

Sanderson サンダーソン

Overall Design:Philippe Starck

Hotel
ホテル

▶ 50 Berners Street, London W1T 3NG
http://www.sandersonlondon.com

Leaflet
リーフレット

Post Card
ポストカード

Sanderson, the second hotel founded by Ian Schrager in London, is an extraordinary "Urban Spa" – the first of its kind – that represents the "Next Wave" of hotel. This breakthrough hotel is a radical, creative and subversive hotel for the new millennium. Sanderson is a magical and serenely elegant sanctuary, a genuine "Oasis" in the midst of one of Europe's busiest, most cosmopolitan cities.

イアン・シュレガーが手がけたホテルではロンドンで2つ目となるサンダーソン。世界初の試みであるこの特別な「アーバン・スパ」はホテル界のニューウェーブ。先進的かつ独創的なこのホテルは新世紀のホテルの先駆けです。幻想的で静謐とした気品ある楽園は、ヨーロッパ最大級の国際都市ロンドンのオアシスとなるでしょう。

St Martin's Lane

セント・マーチンズ・レーン

Overall Design:Philippe Starck   AD:Fabien Baron, Lisa Atkin, Melissa Sison   Graphic Design:Michael Nash Associates
Production Architect:Harper Mackey Ltd

Hotel

ホテル

▶ 45 St. Martin's Lane, London WC2N 4HX
http://www.stmartinslane.com

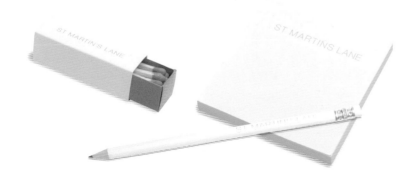

Flyer
フライヤー

From its dazzling location at the hub of Covent Garden, West End theatres and Trafalgar Square, St Martins Lane is a dramatic and daring reinvention of the urban resort. Smart, witty and sophisticated, Philippe Starck's design is a brilliant collision of influences - from the modern to the baroque - that suffuses the hotel with energy, vitality and magic.

コベントガーデン、ウエストエンド・シアター、トラファルガー・スクエアの中間地点というすばらしい立地のこのホテルは、ドラマチックで大胆な革命的アーバンリゾート。機知に富み洗練されたフィリップ・スタルクのデザインは現代からバロックまでのさまざまな要素が織り込まれ、パワーと不思議な魅力にあふれています。

INDEX

Submittors

HOUSING FLYER
ハウジングフライヤー

Page: 288 (256 in Color)　￥14,000＋Tax

全国主要都市から集めた一戸建、分譲マンション、複合住宅などの不動産案内チラシを厳選し約700点を一挙掲載。見る人に物件の完成、住み心地、ライフスタイルを想像させるイメージ写真やイラスト、間取り図、その他情報などを、わかりやすくデザインしたチラシを多数収録します。また物件を紹介したWeb、チラシ制作に役立つＣＧの事例、制作現場からみたチラシの最前線、不動産案内のキャッチコピー集などを加えた盛りだくさんの内容でお届けします。

Some 700 real estate flyers advertising houses, condominium apartments and housing complex collected from major cities throughout Japan brought together in one volume.

SALES STRATEGY AND DESIGN
販売戦略とデザイン

Page: 224 (Full Color)　￥15,000＋Tax

様々な業種の商品発売（サービス業の商品も含む）に伴う告知プロモーションを商品ごとに紹介。思わず手に取るネーミングや、店頭で目を引くパッケージ、消費者の心をくすぐるノベルティなど、各々のアイテムを巧みに利用した例を多数収録。

Unique and outstanding graphic tools in new product/service launching. Here are packages, novelties and the naming of product offering the newest communication styles to consumers!! With explanation of concept and motive for product / promotional tools.

販売戦略とデザインは、切っても切れない関係というのが、この本のあらすじです。

Sales Strategy and Design

HAND-LETTERING UNBOUND
書き文字・装飾文字 グラフィックス

Page: 192 (Full Color)　￥9,800＋Tax

普段使われるフォントではなく、手書きや装飾された個性的な文字を使用したグラフィック作品を紹介。筆文字は力強く和のイメージを、ペン文字はラフでやさしいイメージを感じさせます。文字選びは作品のイメージを左右する重要なポイントです。

A massive collection of free-minded lettering, highlighting eye-catchy handwritings and ornamental writings. All selected works are full of handmade originality, like writings with pen or brush, needlework writings and stitch wrings and more.

2 kilo of KesselsKramer
ケッセルスクライマーの2キロ

Page: 880 (Full Color)　￥9,800＋Tax

ヨーロッパで大評判のケッセルスクライマーの作品とその秘訣を大公開！ よろめくほど重い２キロのコンテンツ。 これを読めば、アムステルダムの小さなクリエイティブ集団がコミュニケーションの世界でヘビー一級になった理由がわかる。

2 kilo of KesselsKramer. Brick or Book? Weighing in at a staggering two kilograms the contents include: - Everything the renowned agency has made. Go to the gym, then try and lift 2 kilo of KesselsKramer. It's the best way to see how this small agency from Amsterdam became a heavyweight in the world of communication.

URBAN SIGN DESIGN
最新 看板・サイン大全集 （CD-ROM付）

Page: 256 (Full Color)　￥15,000＋Tax

街を彩るさまざまな看板を飲食・製造・販売・サービスなど業種別にまとめて紹介。256ページのボリュームに加え、掲載写真の収録CD-ROMも付いた看板デザイン集の決定版。サイン業界のプロから、あらゆるクリエイターにお薦めしたい1冊です。

From among the many signs that flood city streetscapes, we've selected only the most striking, the most beautiful, the most tasteful, and present them here categorized by industry: restaurant, manufacturing, retail, and service. A whopping 256 pages of signs ranging from world-renowned brands to local restaurants, this single volume is sure to provide a source of ideas with a CD-ROM.

NEW SHOP IMAGE GRAPHICS 2
ニュー ショップイメージ グラフィックス 2

Page: 224 (Full Color)　￥15,000＋Tax

お店の個性を強く打ち出すためには、販売戦略と明確なコンセプトに基づいた、ショップのイメージ作りが重要です。本書は様々な業種からデザイン性の高いショップアイデンティティ展開を、グラフィックツールと店舗写真、コンセプト文を交え紹介。

Second volume of the best seller titls in overseas. New Shop Image Graphics released in 2002. This book covers the latest, unique and impressive graphics in interiors and exteriors of various shops as well as their supporting materials.

WORLD BUSINESS CARDS TODAY
世界発 最新名刺のデザイン

Page: 208 (Full Color)　￥5,800＋Tax

世界中から厳選された、デザイン性に優れた名刺・ショップカードを特集。海外のデザイナーをはじめ、サービス業や製造業、ブティックや飲食店など幅広い職種の名刺を多数掲載。ひと目見たら忘れない、印象に残る名刺が詰まった1冊です。

Humdrum business cards, good-bye! Feast your eyes on the numerous unforgettable examples of business cards that transcend language and nationality to convey the character of the individuals they represent and the spirit of their businesses. The definitive source book of design making optimal use of limited space.

PROGRESSIVE DIRECT MAIL
ワールド DM エキスポ

Page: 160 (Full Color)　￥7,800＋Tax

世界各地から届いた個性あふれるすばらしい作品が集結！ページをめくるごとに感動の作品に出会える。シャープでクール・ユニークでおもしろい・思わず微笑んでしまう愛らしい作品など、多種多様な作品があなたに刺激を与えます。

A collection of distinctive and wonder-filled direct-mail pieces from all corners of the world; each turn of the page packs a surprise! The variety of works - from the sharp and cool to the unique, funny, and even charming, which inadvertently bring smiles to your face - tickle the intellect and the emotions in a multitude of ways. This must-have single volume is a treasure trove of inspiration.

NEW MAIL ORDER GRAPHICS

最新 通販グラフィックス

Page: 208 (Full Color)　￥14,000+Tax

最新の通販カタログと通販WEBの特集です。デザインが機能的で秀逸なもの、コンテンツがユニークなものなど、多様なアプローチを見せる通販ツールの現在形を、衣料品・食品・美容・健康などにコンテンツわけし、紹介しています。

The latest catalog and website designs for mail ordering services, featuring not only the pages for products/services but also those for ordering forms. Well-designed pages must inspire your new images for original creativities.

ADVERTISING PHOTOGRAPHY IN JAPAN 2006

年鑑 日本の広告写真2006

Page: 240 (Full Color)　￥14,500+Tax

気鋭の広告写真をそろえた（社）日本広告写真家協会（APA）の監修による本年鑑は、日本の広告界における最新のトレンドと、その証言者たる作品を一堂に見られる貴重な資料として、国内外の広告に携わる方にとって欠かせない存在です。

A spirited collection of works comppiled under the editorial supervision of the Japan Advertising Photographers' Association (APA) as its 11th issue. Presenting the latest works by freshest talent in Japanese advertising world.

COSMETICS PACKAGE DESIGN

コスメパッケージ＆ボトル デザイン

Page: 160 (Full Color)　￥7,800+Tax

化粧品、ヘルスケア用品（シャンプー・石鹸・入浴剤・整髪剤）のパッケージ、ボトルやチューブのデザインを中心に紹介。また、それらの商品しおり、ディスプレイ写真もあわせて掲載。「今、女性にウケるデザインとは？」がわかる1冊です。

Cosmetics and personal care products and their packaging represent the state of the art in design sensitive to the tastes of contemporary women. This collection presents a wide range of flowery, elegant, charming, and unique packages for makeup, skincare, body, bath, and hair-care products and fragrances selected from all over the world.

PRINT & WEB CATALOG

プリント＆Web カタログ

Page: 288 (Full Color)　￥14,000+Tax

商品を魅力的に見せる、紙カタログとWebの商品案内ページを紹介します。図を使いわかりやすく表現した作品、ひときわ楽しく工夫された作品、商品の一覧が見やすい作品など、消費者の購買意欲を刺激するカタログを多数掲載しています。

A collection introducing printed catalogs and Web pages that show products off to their advantage in attractive and interesting ways. Works that use illustrations to make product characteristics readily understood, works that use devices to make them above all fun, works with products lists that are easy on the eye...the many catalogs presented within have one feature in common: they excite and stimulate consumer interest.

365 DAYS OF NEWSPAPER INSERTS　Autumn / Winter Edition

365日の折込チラシ大百科 秋冬編

Page: 240 (Full Color)　￥13,000+Tax

紅葉の行楽・運動会・お月見・ハロウィン・クリスマス・御歳暮・忘年会など、 生活に密着した季節のセール案内を多数収録！デザイン性の高さはもちろんのこと、斬新な企画やアイデア、優れたキャッチコピーの作品を厳選して紹介しています。

A collection of latest newspaper inserts in Japan of various retailers. The works include sales promotional inserts for the seasonal occasions such as Halloween, Viewing Scarlet maple leaves, Sports festival, Christmas, and so on. Well-designed works with eye-catching copies are inspirational resources for all designers and advertising creators.

365 DAYS OF NEWSPAPER INSERTS　Spring / Summer Edition

365日の折込チラシ大百科 春夏編

Page: 240 (Full Color)　￥13,000+Tax

全国の主要6都市から厳選された春夏の新聞折込チラシを一挙に掲載。優れたデザインや配色、目を引くキャッチコピーの作品が満載。お正月、成人の日、バレンタイン、お雛様、子供の日、母の日、父の日などの作品を含む季節感溢れる1冊です。

Volume 3 of our popular series! Eye-catching newspaper inserts – outstanding in design, color and copywriting – selected from 6 major Japanese cities between January and June. Brimming with the spirit and events of spring: New Year's, Valentine's Day, Girls'/Boys' Days, Mother's/Father's Days, and more.

LOCAL COLOR GRAPHICS

地方色豊かなローカルグラフィックス

Page: 224 (Full Color)　￥14,000+Tax

タウン誌や広報誌、土産物・飲食店・観光案内のパンフレット・ポスター、美術館や各自治体のイベントポスター、特産品のパッケージなど、地方で頒布されているデザインの優れたグラフィックスを、全国9地方に分類し紹介しています。

Well-designed graphic works for promoting local foods & goods, events, tourism in leaflets and magazines for towns, pamphlets and posters for souvenirs, restaurants or sightseeing. More than 250 works are layouted by legion in Japan.

NEW TYPOGRAPHICS WITH FONT SAMPLES

ニュー タイポグラフィックス 書体見本付

Page: 168 (128 in Color)　￥7,800+Tax

近年開発されてきたデジタリックなフォントを使用したグラフィック作品の特集。日本だけでなくヨーロッパやアメリカなど世界中から、クオリティが高く、ビジュアルアピールの強い作品を厳選して収録。巻末にフォントの書体見本を掲載しています。

Newest and exciting collection of typography from all over the world featuring graphic design with brand-new digital fonts. You can also easily refer to the samples of the fonts used in the works at the end of the book. Including commercial font, custom font, free font and more.

THE BEST INFORMATIONAL DIAGRAMS 2

ベスト インフォメーショナル ダイアグラム 2

Page: 232 (Full Color)　¥14,000+Tax

グラフ・チャート・地図など、複雑な情報をわかりやすく視覚化して人々に伝達することを目的として制作されたビジュアル・グラフィックスを多数収録。海外クリエイターの作品を中心に、最新の秀作を一挙に紹介しています。

Graphs, charts, maps, schematics... a collection of the latest in graphics that visualize complex information thus making it easy to comprehend. This wide range of diagram masterpieces from around the world documents the state of the art.

OUTSTANDING SMALL PAMPHLET GRAPHICS

街で目立つ小型パンフレット

Pages: 240 (Full Color)　¥14,000+Tax

街やショップの店頭で手に入る無料の小型パンフ。50ヶ所以上の街で集めた約1,000点から、販売促進ツールとして効果的に機能している作品を厳選。衣・食・住・遊の業種別に分類し機能的で美しい小型パンフレットを約250点紹介します。

250 small-scale pamphlets selected for their beauty and function as effective sales promotional tools from roughly 1000 pieces available to customers at more than 50 locations. Grouped for valuable reference by type of business type under the categories: Food, Clothing, Shelter, and Entertainment.

WORLD CATALOG EXPO

ワールド カタログ エキスポ

Page: 192 (Full Color)　¥5,800+Tax

一目でわかるように、衣食住のコンテンツは色分けされています。高級感あるスマートな作品、楽しくカラフルな作品、斬新なアイデアの作品など、ページをめくるごとに様々な作品の個性が広がる、国際色豊かな1冊です。

A survey of outstanding catalogs from around the world: simple and refined, colorful and playful, full of novel ideas. Color-coded for easy identification under the categories: Fashion, Food, and Living. Highly original works, international in flavor, spill out with each turn of the page.

WORLD CORPORATE PROFILE GRAPHICS

ニュー世界の会社案内グラフィックス

Page: 256 (Full Color)　¥14,000+Tax

世界から集めた最新の会社案内・学校・施設案内とアニュアルレポートを業種別に紹介。作品を大きく見せながらも形態、デザイン制作コンセプト、コンテンツ内容を簡潔に掲載しています。世界のデザイナーの動向を掴む上でも貴重な1冊です。

The latest exemplary company, school and institution guides and annual reports collected from diversified industries worldwide and grouped by line of business. Shown large scale, the pieces are accompanied by brief descriptions of their content and the concepts behind their design. Valuable for gleaning the latest trends in corporate communications.

HOUSE ADVERTISING GRAPHICS

ハウス アドバタイジング グラフィックス

Page: 240 (Full Color)　¥15,000+Tax

不動産広告を中心に、建材などの広告や、キッチンやバスなどの室内設備に関する広告など、「住まい」にまつわるグラフィックを一挙掲載。デザイン性が高いパンフレット・折り込みチラシ・DMなどの販促ツールを一望できます。

A collection of advertising related to real estate – unique building materials, kitchen/bath equipment, architectural features – centered around "the home". This single volume of well-designed pamphlets, newspaper inserts, direct-mail and more provides an overview of state-of-the-art sales promotional tools associated with housing.

FOOD SHOP GRAPHICS

フード ショップ グラフィックス

Page: 224 (Full Color)　¥14,000+Tax

レストラン・カフェ・菓子店など、国内外のオリジナリティ溢れる飲食店のショップアイデンティティ特集です。メニューやリーフレットなどのグラフィックと、内装・外装の店舗写真、コンセプト文を交え、約120店を紹介。

Restaurants, cafes, sweet shops... 120 of the world's most original food-related store identities. Together with graphic applications ranging from menus to matches, each presentation features exterior and interior photos of the shops and brief descriptions of the concepts behind them.

GRAND OPENING GRAPHICS

オープン ツール グラフィックス

Pages: 216 (Full Color)　¥14,000+Tax

ショップや施設をオープンする際に制作するグラフィックツールは、新しい「空間」のイメージを消費者へ伝える大切な役割を果たします。本書ではオープン時に制作された案内状やショップツール、店舗写真などを業種ごとに多数収録。

The graphic applications created for the openings of new stores and facilities play a critical role in conveying store image to customers. Categorized by line of business, this book presents the wide range of graphics — from invitations to in-store collateral — that form the first impressions in building strategic store identity.

DESIGN IDEAS WITH LIMITED COLOR

限られた色のデザインアイデア

Page: 208 (192 in Color)　¥13,000+Tax

限られた刷り色で効果的にデザインされた作品を、使用された刷り色の色見本・パントーン（DIC含む）ナンバーと併せて紹介。色の掛け合わせと濃度変化がわかるカラーチャートを併載。無限大のアイデアを探し出すときに必要となる1冊。

A collection of the latest graphic works effectively reproduced using limited ink colors. Presented with color swatches and the Pantone/DIC numbers of the ink colors used, gradation and duotone works also feature simple color charts indicating screen and density changes. A reference of limitless ideas for anyone specifying color.

ENVIRONMENTAL COMMUNICATION GRAPHICS

環境コミュニケーションツール グラフィックス

Page: 224 (Full Color)　¥14,000+Tax

環境リポートや、環境をテーマとしたリーフレット、チラシ、ポスターなど、環境コミュニケーション・ツールを一堂に会し、業種別に紹介します。本書は、会社案内や各種パンフレット制作などあらゆるクリエイティブのアイデアソースとしても、利用価値の高い1冊です。

This book provides an overview of environmental communications tools, including leaflets, handbills and posters that focus on the topic of the environment, classifying them by type of business. This book is indeed a valuable source of creative ideas that graphic artists can use in creating company brochures and many other brochures.

SCHOOL & FACILITY PROSPECTUS GRAPHICS

学校・施設案内 グラフィックス

Pages: 224 (Full Color)　¥15,000+Tax

「学校」「施設」という2つの大きなコンテンツを軸に、デザイン、企画、コンセプトに優れたカタログ、リーフレットなどの案内ツールを収録。表紙、中ページのレイアウト、構成からキャッチコピーまで見やすく紹介しています。

A collection presenting examples of well-designed and conceptually outstanding guides (catalogs, pamphlets, leaflets, etc) focusing on two broad categories: schools and service facilities. Documentation includes cover and inside pages, highlighting layout, composition, and catch copy.

ENCYCLOPEDIA OF PAPER-FOLDING DESIGN

DM・カードの折り方デザイン集

Page: 256 (B/W)　¥5,800+Tax

1枚の紙を折ることにより平面とは違う表情が生まれ、新しい機能を備えることが出来ます。DMやカードの折り方デザイン250点の作例と展開図とともに、その折りを効果的に生かした実際の作品も参考例として紹介。永久保存版の1冊です。

Folding a single sheet of paper imbues it with another dimension, and can change it in function. More than 250 printed materials shown as they are effected by folding, together with flat diagrams of their prefolded forms. The very reference material designers collect, permanently preserved in a single volume.

ENVIRONMENT/WELFARE-RELATED GRAPHICS

環境・福祉 グラフィックス

Pages: 240 (Full Color)　¥15,000+Tax

環境保全への配慮が世界的な常識となりつつある今日、企業も積極的に環境・福祉など社会的テーマを中心にした広告キャンペーンを展開しています。国内外の優れた環境・福祉広告を紹介した本書は今後の広告を考えるために必携の1冊となるでしょう。

Environmental conservation is now a worldwide concern, and corporate advertising campaigns based on environmental and social themes are on the rise. This collection of noteworthy local and international environment/welfare-related publicity is an essential reference for anyone involved in the planning and development of future advertising.

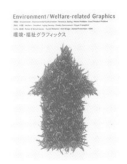

PACKAGE & WRAPPING GRAPHICS

パッケージ & ラッピングツール グラフィックス

Page: 224 (Full Color)　¥14,000+Tax

様々な商品パッケージには、販売対象やブランドイメージに沿ったデザイン戦略がなされており、商品イメージを決定する重要な役割を担っています。本書は世界中からデザイン性の高いパッケージとラッピングツールを多数ピックアップし、食・美容・住にコンテンツわけして紹介しています。

Package is based on carefully developed design strategies to appeal to target customers and to build brand and protect image. This collection presents a wide variety of packages and wrapping materials from around the world reflecting the state of the art. It is grouped loosely under the categories food, beauty and living.

NEW ENCYCLOPEDIA OF PAPER-FOLDING DESIGNS

折り方大全集　カタログ・DM編 (CD-ROM付)

Page: 240 (160 in Color)　¥7,800+Tax

デザインの表現方法の1つとして使われている『折り』。日頃何げなく目にしているDMやカード、企業のプロモーション用カタログなど身近なデザイン中に表現されている『折り』から、たたむ機能やせり出す、たわめる機能まで、約200点の作品を展開図で示し、『折り』を効果的に生かした実際の作品を掲載しています。

More than 200 examples of direct mail, cards, and other familiar printed materials featuring simple / multiple folds, folding up, and insertion shown as they are effected by folding along with flat diagrams of their prefolded forms. With CD-ROM.

カタログ・新刊のご案内について

総合カタログ、新刊案内をご希望の方は、はさみ込みのアンケートはがきをご返送いただくか、下記ピエ・ブックスへご連絡下さい。

CATALOGS and INFORMATION ON NEW PUBLICATIONS

If you would like to receive a free copy of our general catalog or details of our new publications, please fill out the enclosed postcard and return it to us by mail or fax.

CATALOGUES ET INFORMATIONS SUR LES NOUVELLES PUBLICATIONS

Si vous désirez recevoir un exemplaire qratuit de notre catalogue généralou des détails sur nos nouvelles publication. veuillez compléter la carte réponse incluse et nous la retourner par courrierou par fax.

CATALOGE und INFORMATIONEN ÜBER NEUE TITLE

Wenn Sie unseren Gesamtkatalog oder Detailinformationen über unsere neuen Titel wünschen.fullen Sie bitte die beigefügte Postkarte aus und schicken Sie sie uns per Post oder Fax.

ピエ・ブックス

〒170-0005　東京都豊島区南大塚2-32-4
TEL: 03-5395-4811　FAX: 03-5395-4812
www.piebooks.com

PIE BOOKS

2-32-4 Minami-Otsuka Toshima-ku Tokyo 170-0005 JAPAN
TEL：+81-3-5395-4811　FAX：+81-3-5395-4812
www.piebooks.com

ショップイメージ グラフィックス イン ロンドン
Shop Image Graphics in London

2007年2月11日　初版第1刷発行
2008年1月13日　初版第2刷発行

Art Direction & Cover Design
セキユリヲ（エア）　Yurio Seki (ea)

Designer
松村大輔　Daisuke Matsumura

Editor
高橋かおる　Kaoru Takahashi

Editor & Coordinator (London)
寺島彩子　Ayako Terashima

Photographers (In Alphabetical Order)
ブレント・ダービー　Brent Darby
中尾健一　Kenichi Nakao
杉浦由紀　Yuki Sugiura
渡部明子　Akiko Watanabe

Translators
白倉三紀子　Mikiko Shirakura
パメラ・三木　Pamela Miki

Illustrator
升ノ内朝子　Asako Masunouchi

Publisher
三芳伸吾　Shingo Miyoshi

発行元　ピエ・ブックス
〒170-0005　東京都豊島区南大塚2-32-4
編集　TEL: 03-5395-4820 FAX: 03-5395-4821
　　　e-mail: editor@piebooks.com
営業　TEL: 03-5395-4811 FAX: 03-5395-4812
　　　e-mail: sales@piebooks.com
http://www.piebooks.com

印刷・製本　株式会社サンニチ印刷

©2007 PIE BOOKS
Printed in Japan
ISBN978-4-89444-583-3 C3070